Preface

- 100 2D CAD Exercises.
- 50 3D CAD Exercises.
- <u>Download original 150 CAD (DWG) files</u> from cadin360.com
- Each exercise can be designed on any CAD software such as AutoCAD, SolidWorks, Catia, PTC Creo Parametric, Siemens NX, Autodesk Inventor and other.
- These exercises are designed to help you test out your basic CAD skills.
- Each exercise can be assigned separately.
- No exercise is a prerequisite for another.
- All dimensions are in mm.

Disclaimer

The book contains 100 2D and 50 3D exercises to enable you practice what you learn. The exercises range from easy to expert level. These exercises are not tutorials. It is a practice book. You can use these exercises to improve your skills in any CAD software. You can download 100 2D CAD & 50 3D DWG files from www.cadin360.com

No part of this publication may be reproduced, stored in a retrieval system or transmitted in any form or
By any means electronic, mechanical, photocopying, recording or sold in whole or in part in any form, otherwise without the prior written Permission of the author & www.cadin360.com
All trademarks and registered trademarks appearing in this guide are the property of their respective owners.

✓ Click to download original 150 CAD (DWG) files
   from **www.cadin360.com**

2D EXERCISES

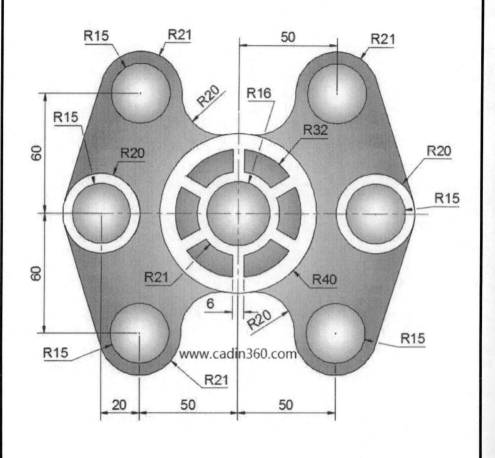

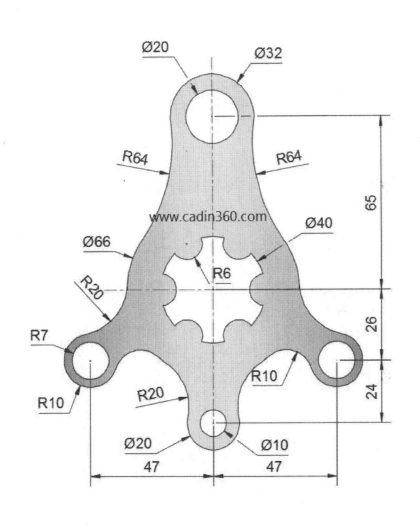

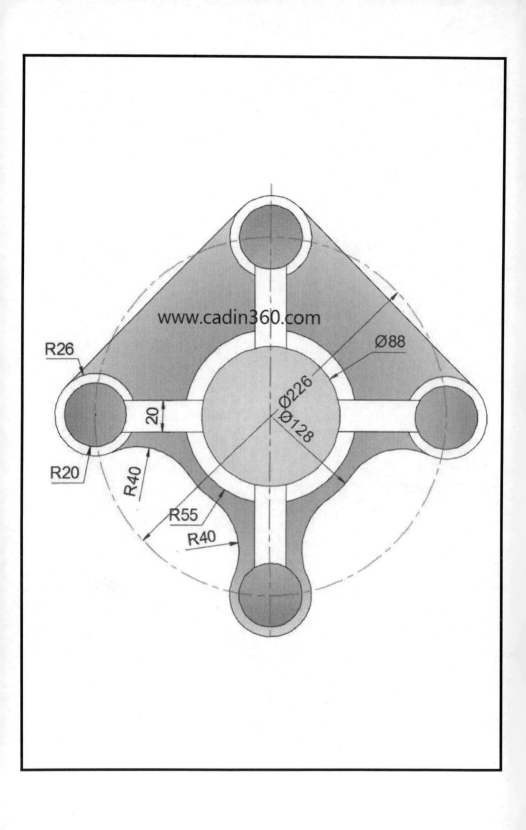

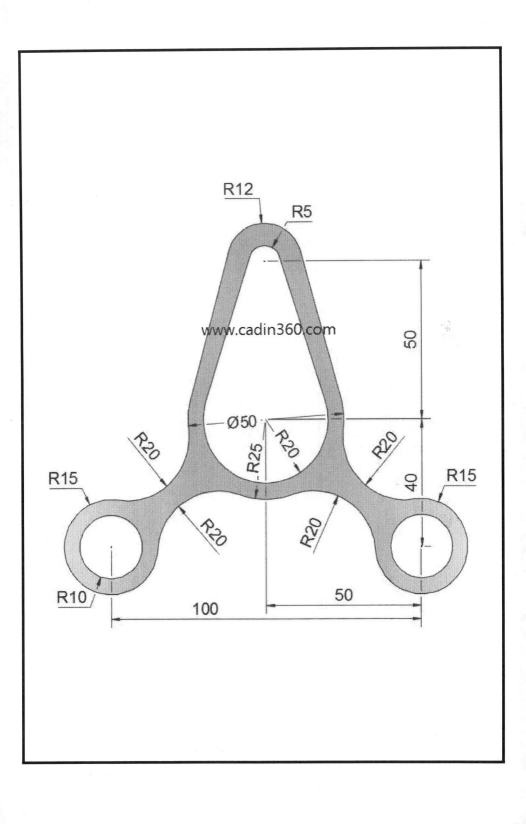

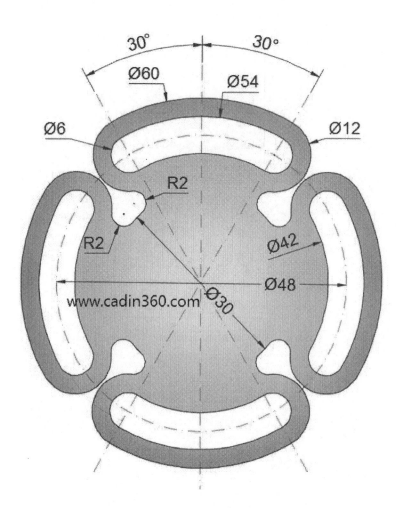

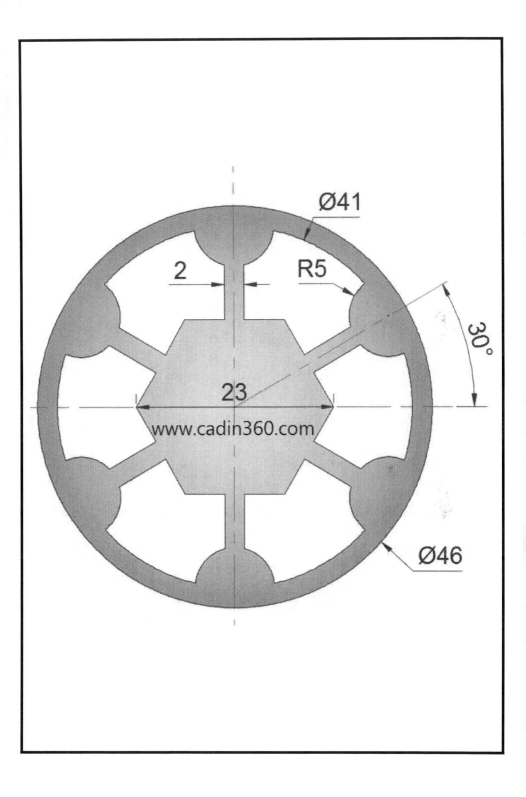

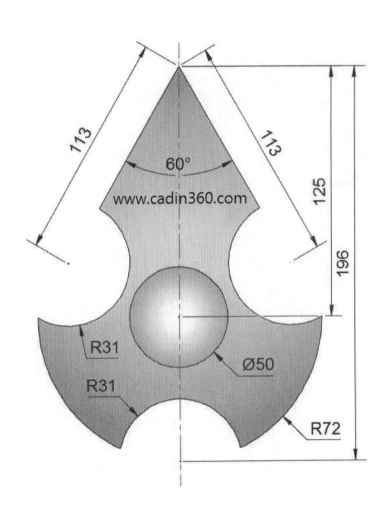

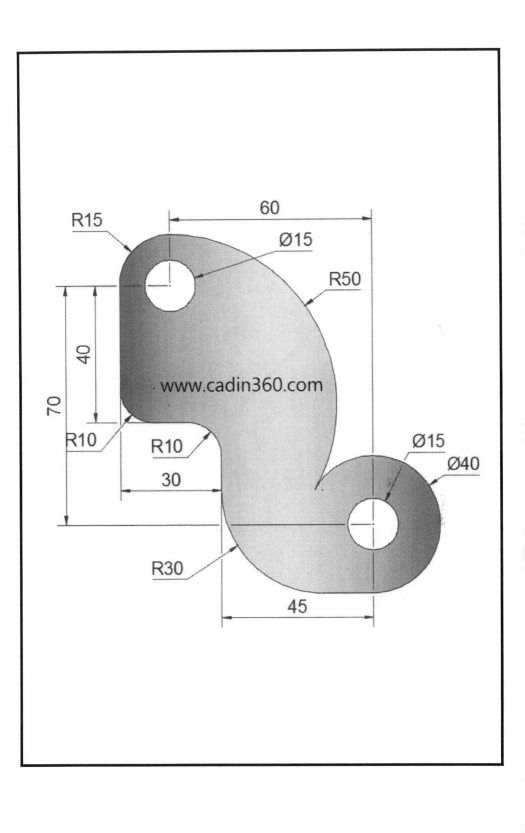

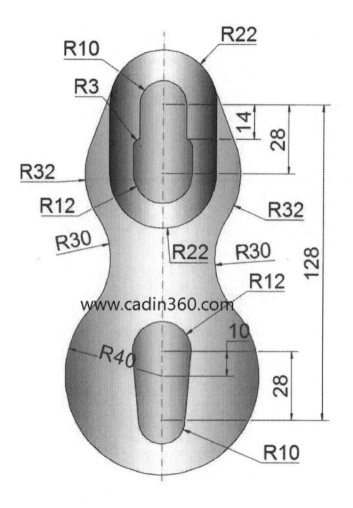

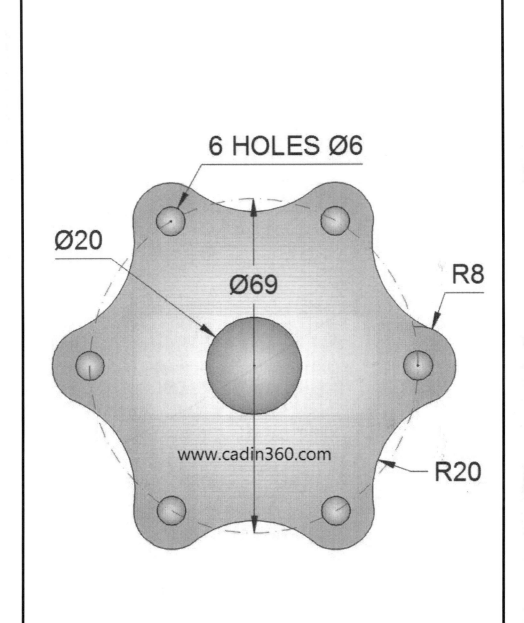

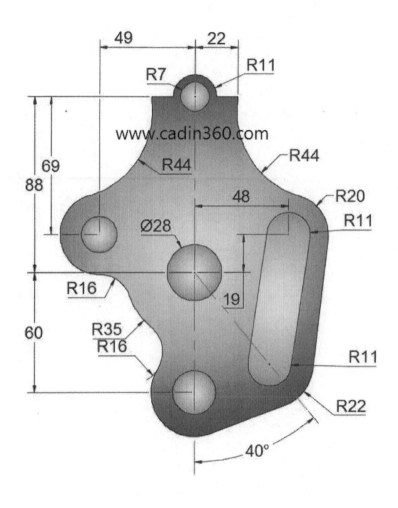

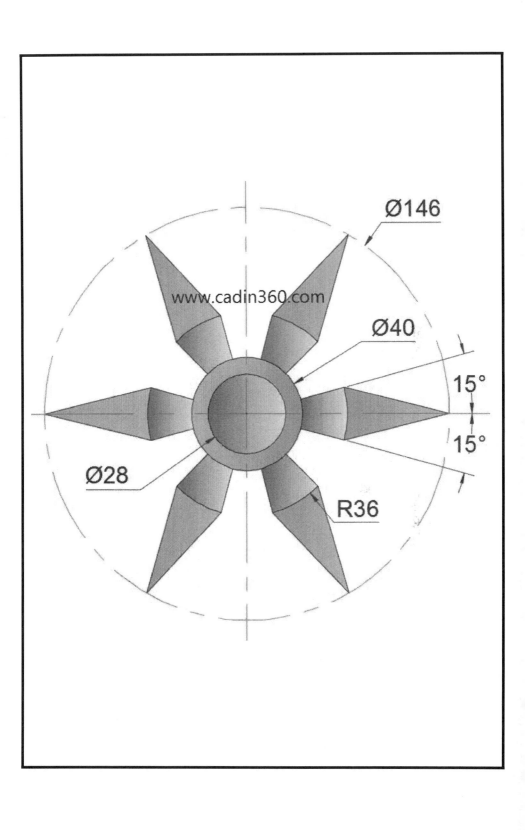

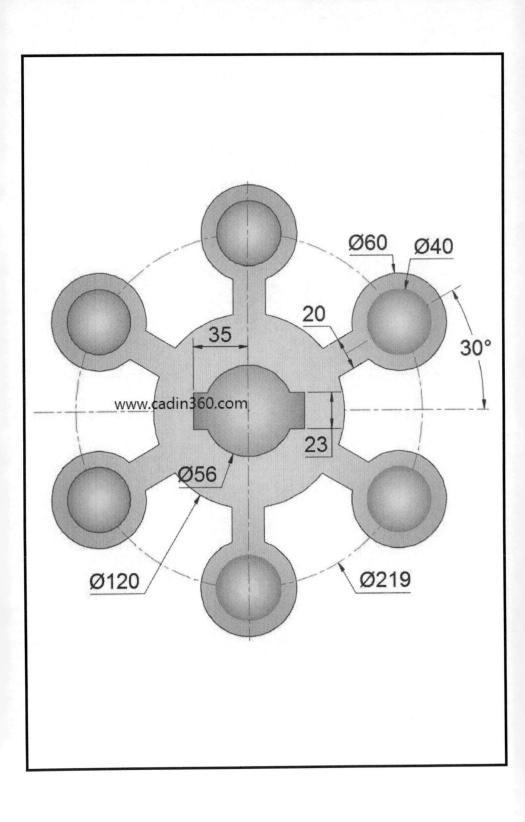

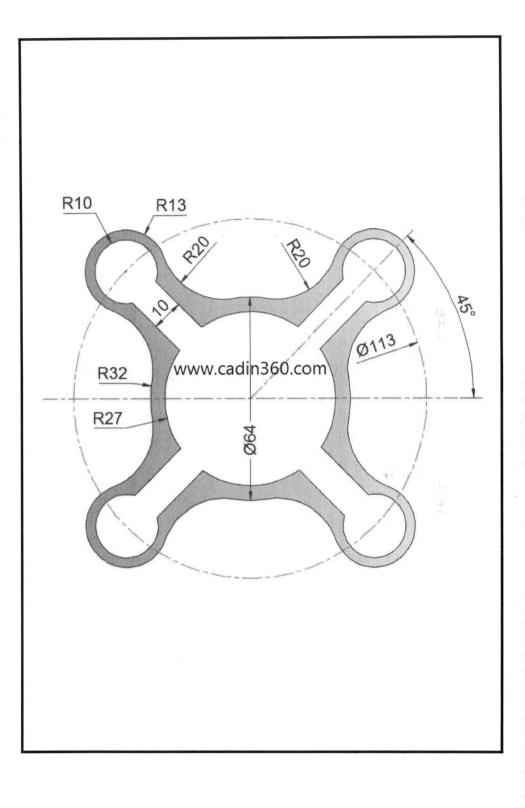

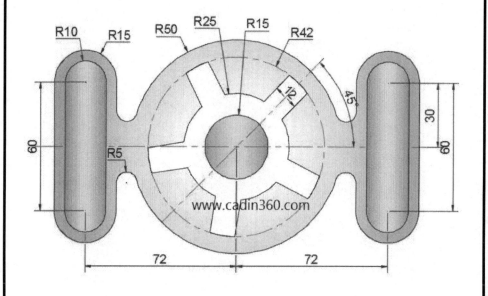

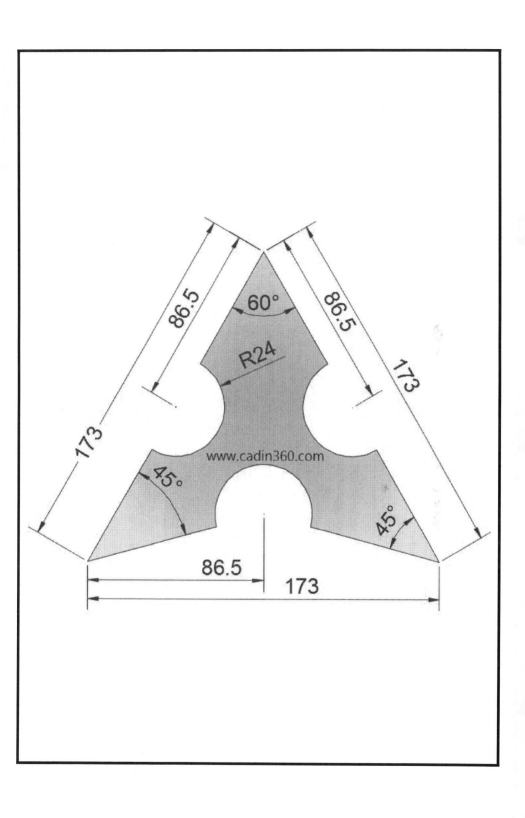

www.cadin360.com

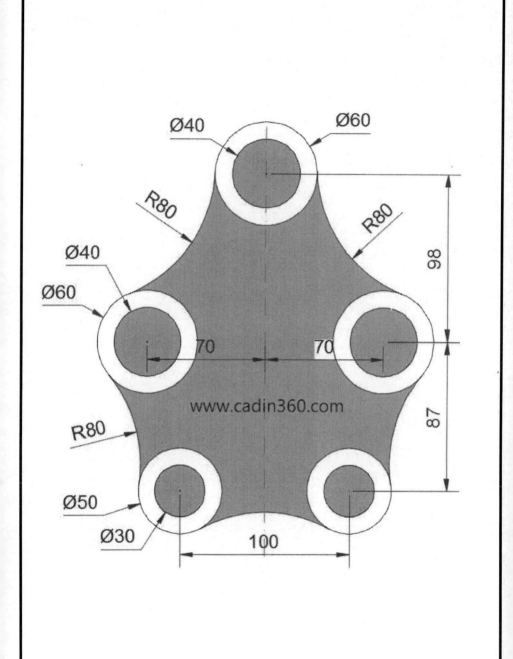

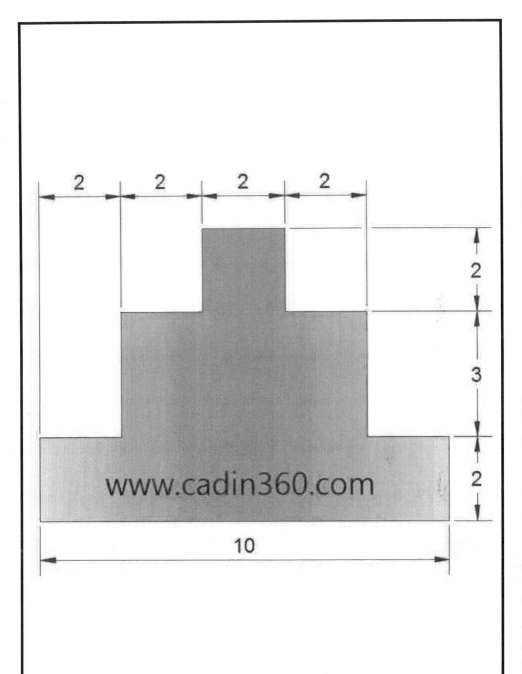

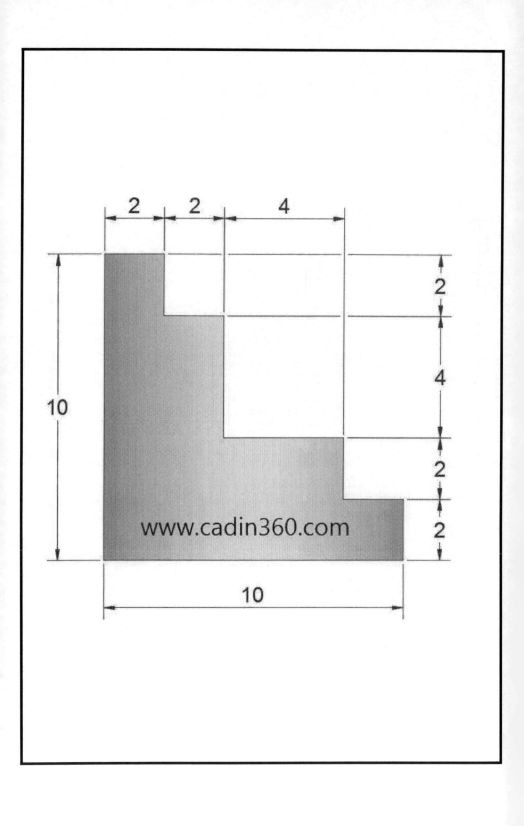

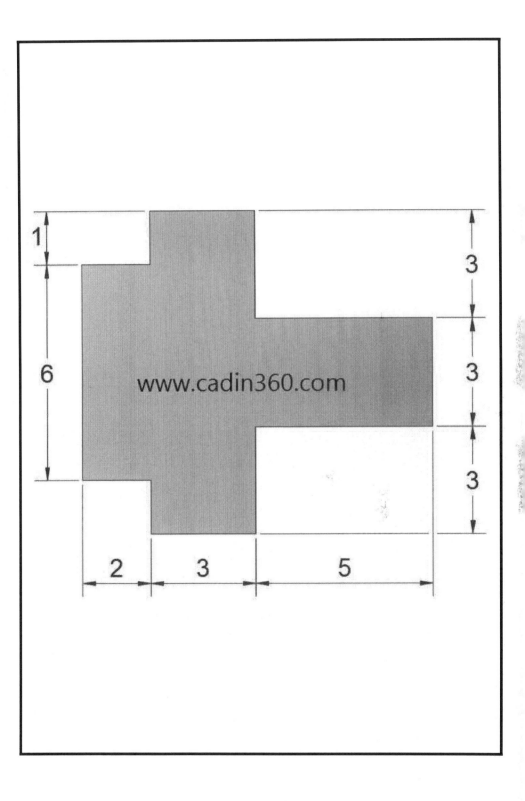

www.cadin360.com

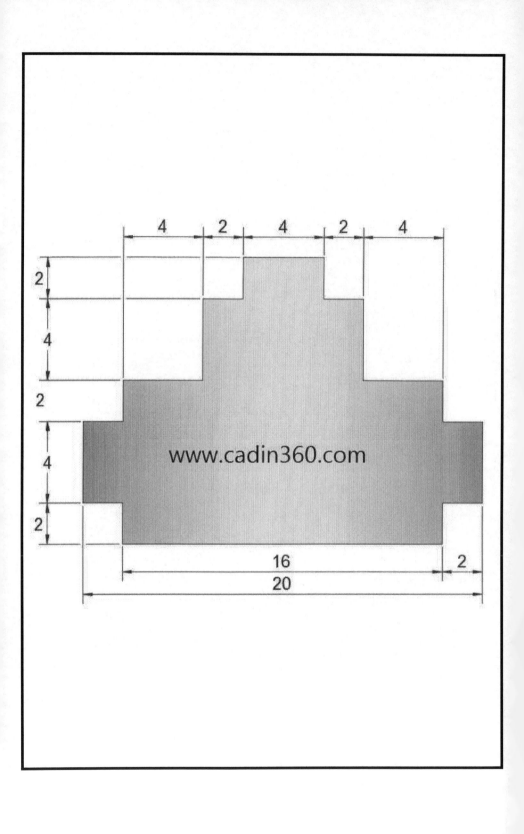

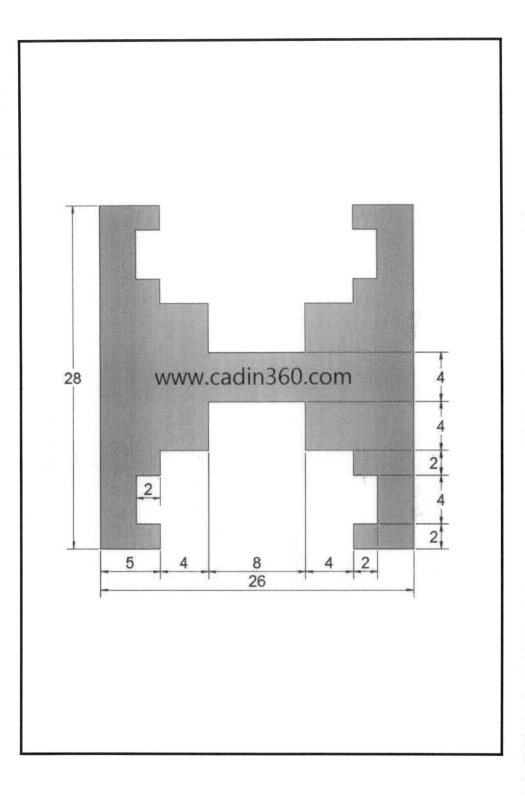

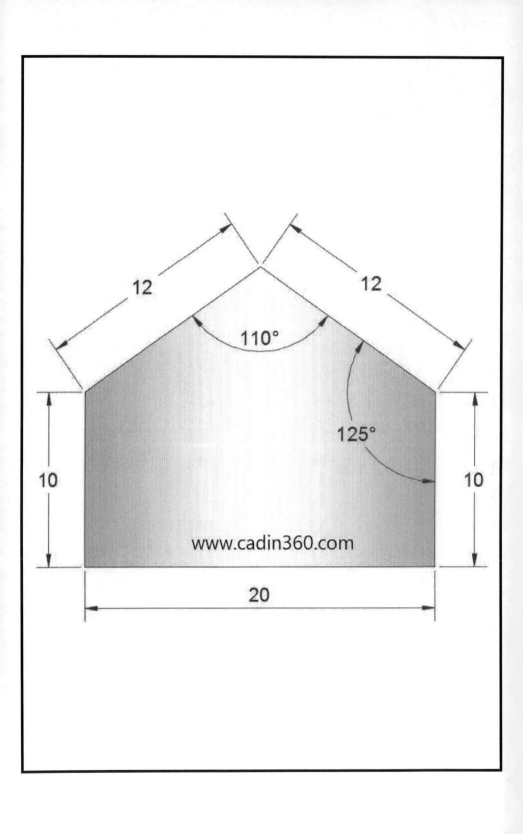

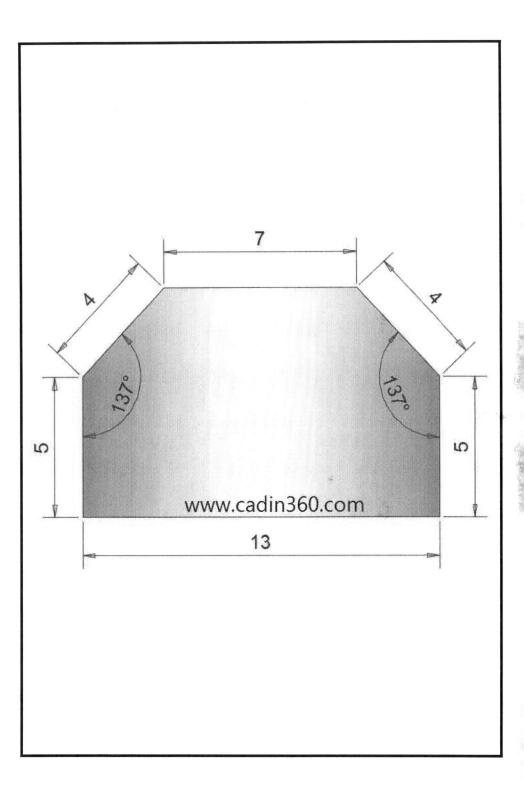

7

4

4

137°

137°

5

5

www.cadin360.com

13

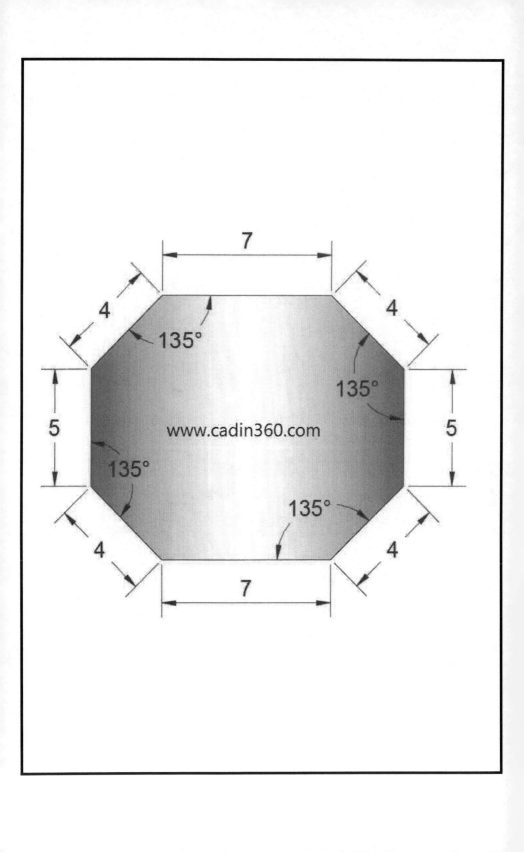

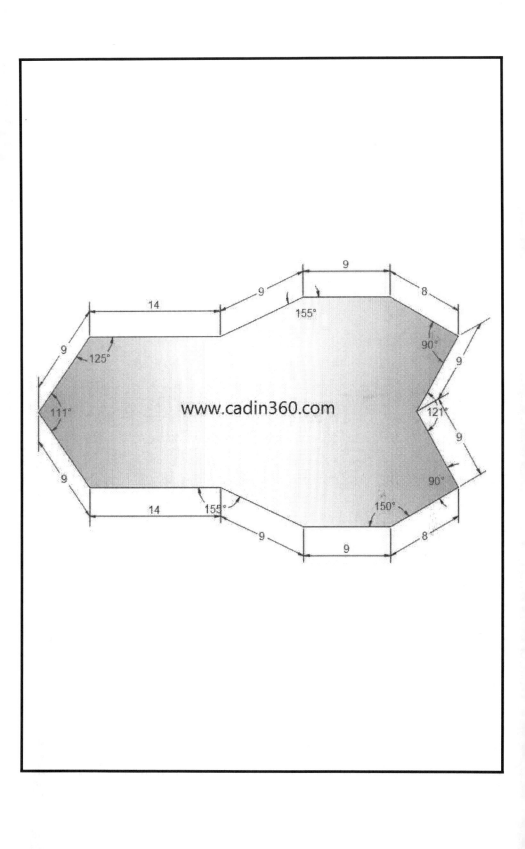

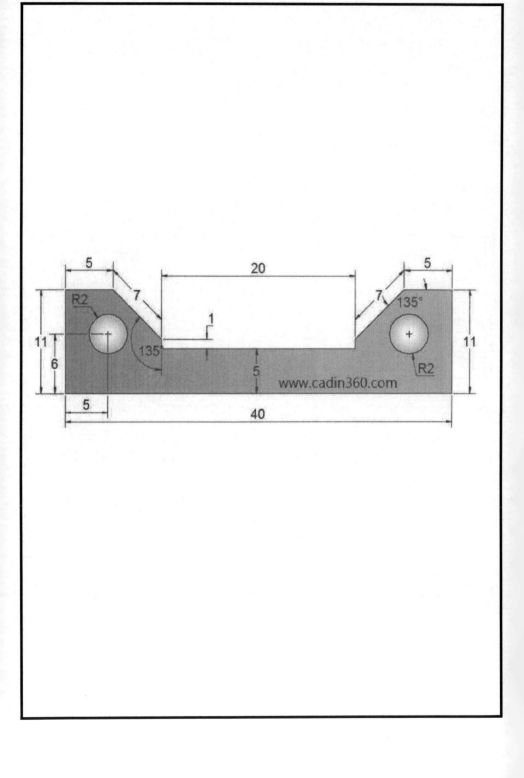

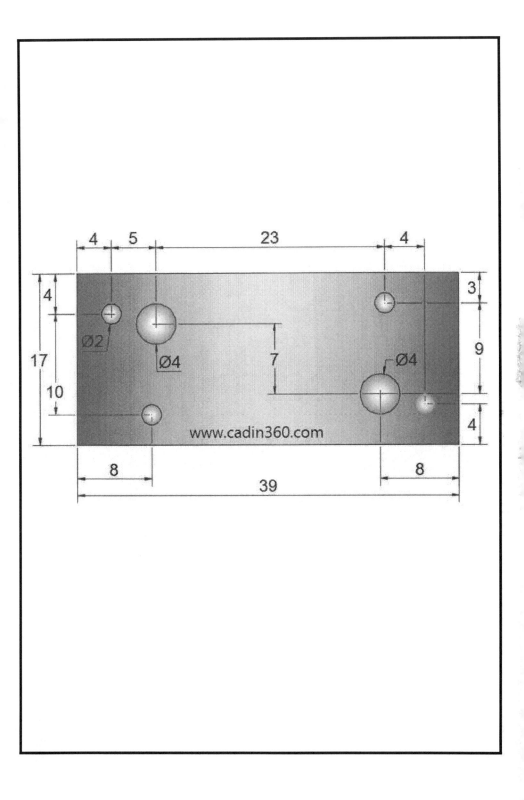

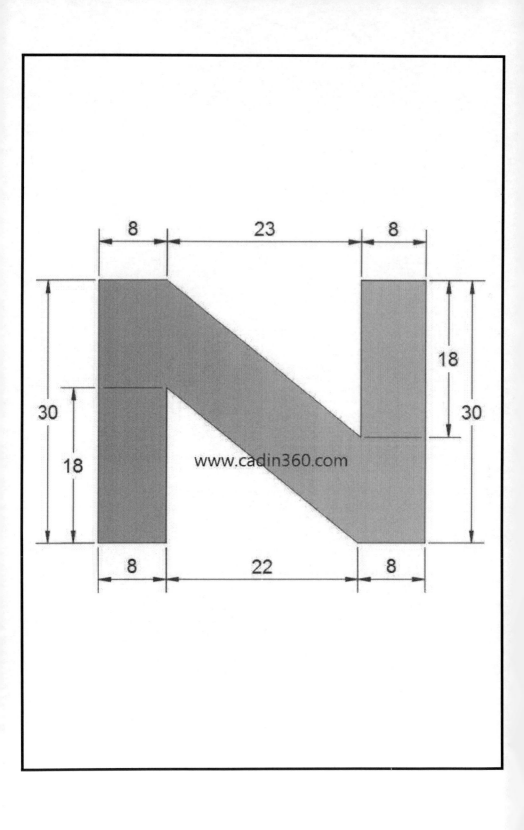

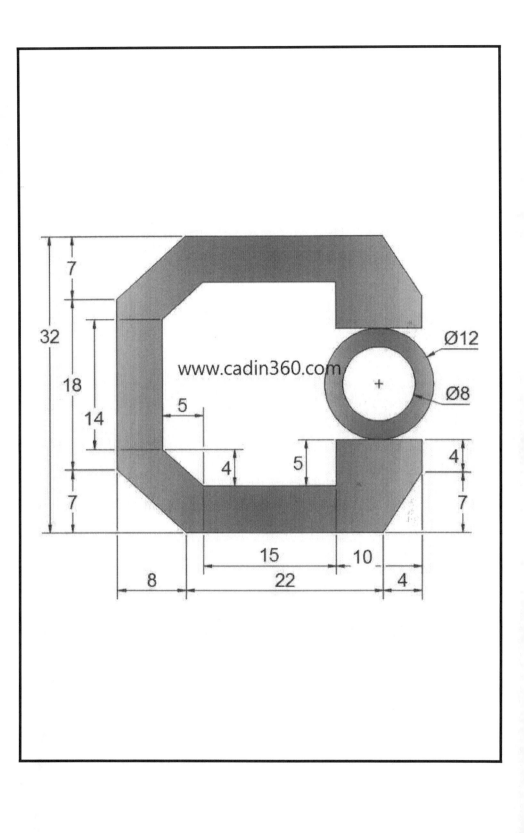

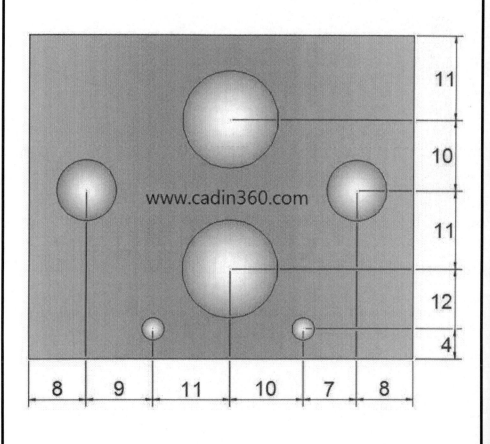

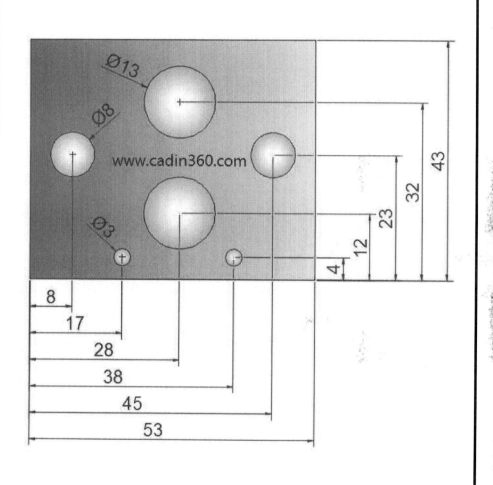

www.cadin360.com

Ø13
Ø8
Ø3

43
32
23
12
4

8
17
28
38
45
53

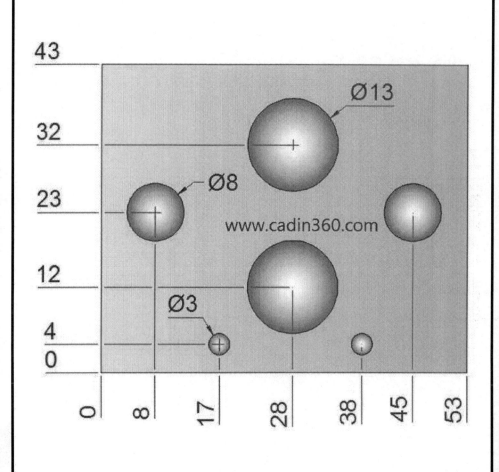

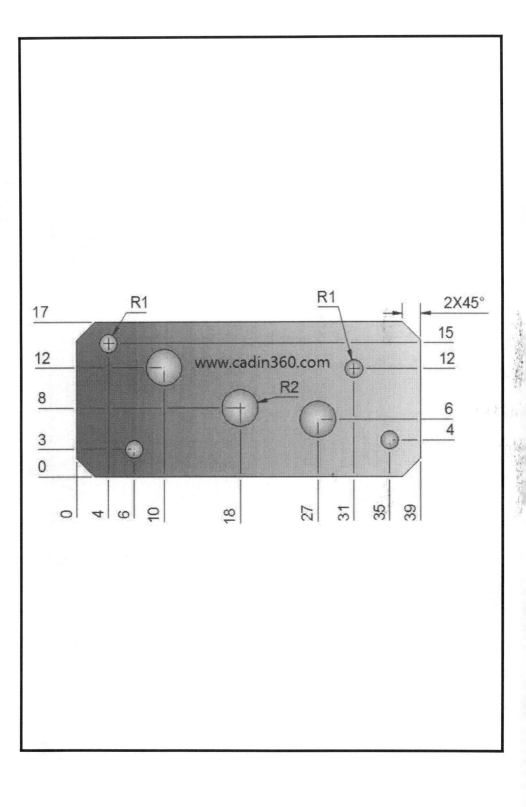

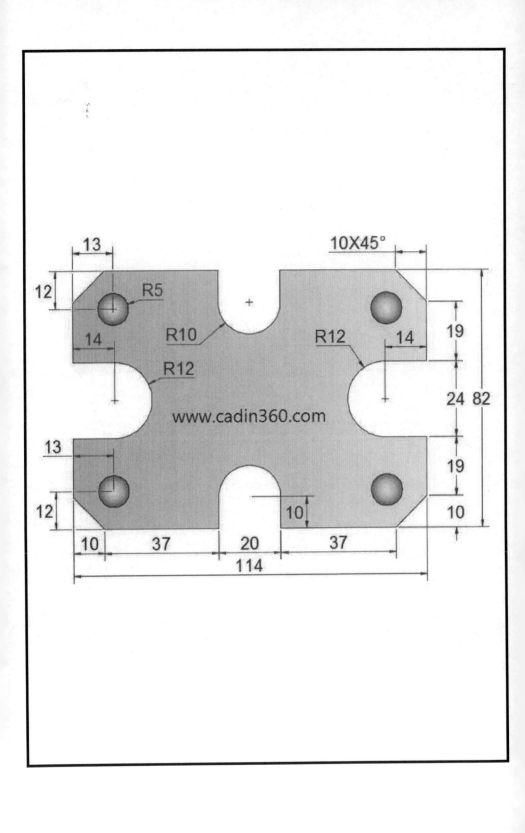

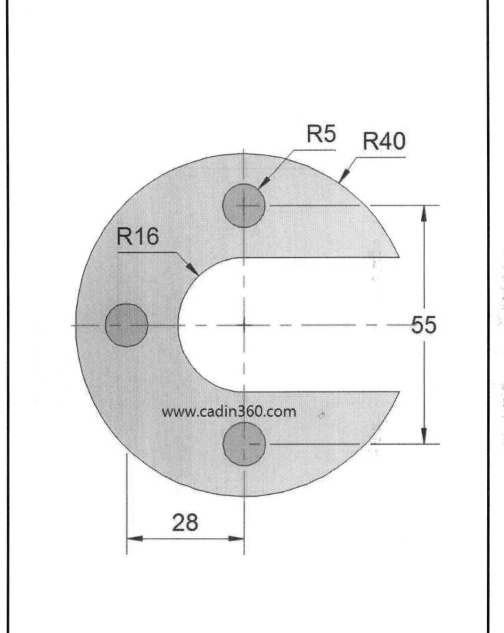

R5   R40

R16

55

28

www.cadin360.com

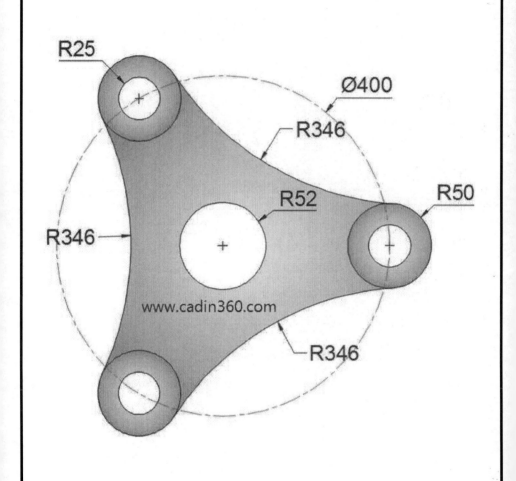

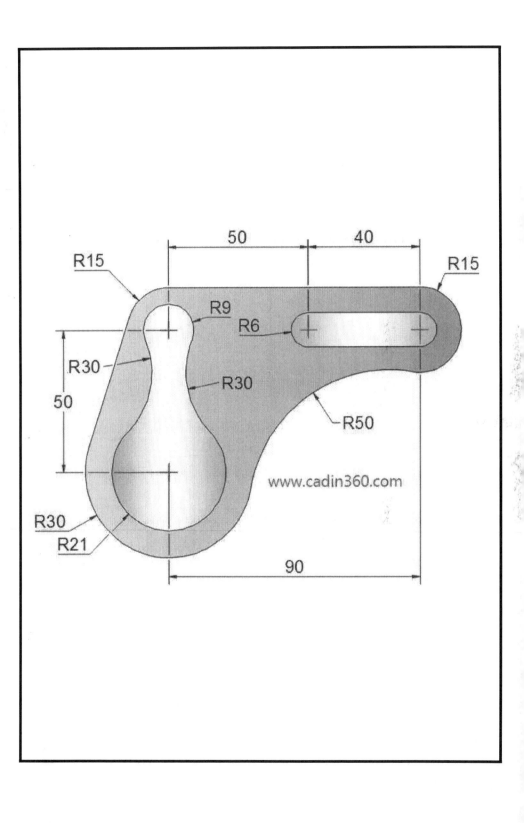

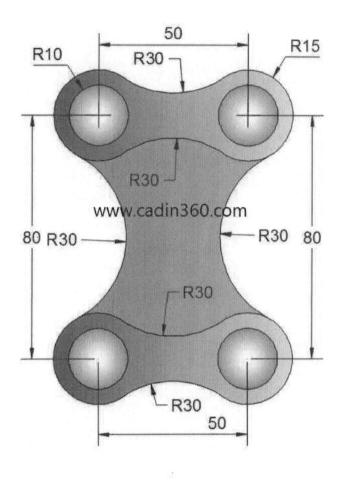

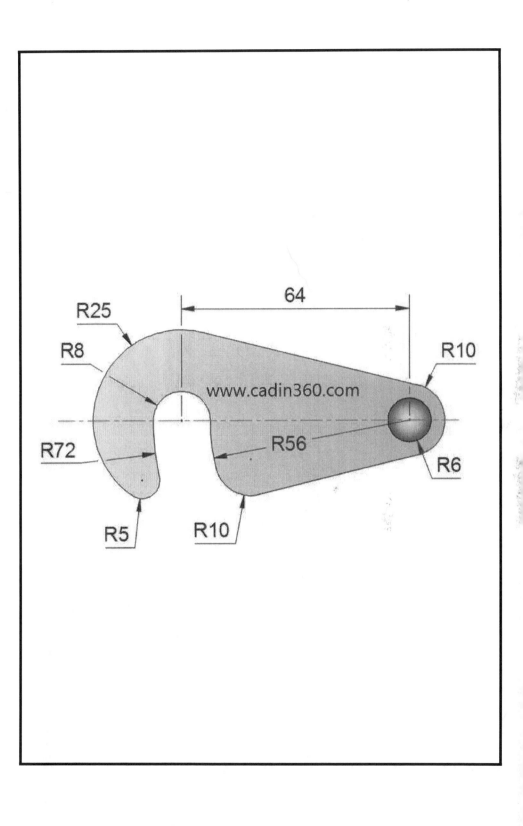

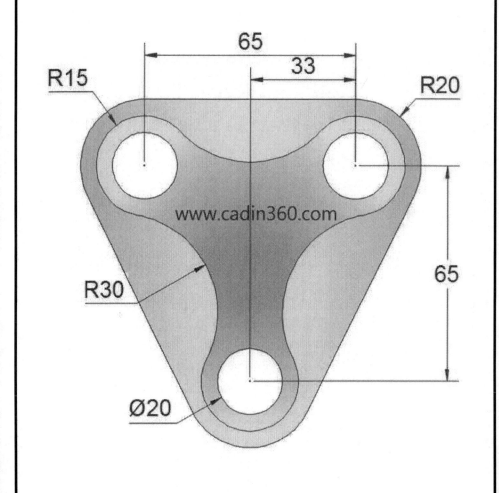

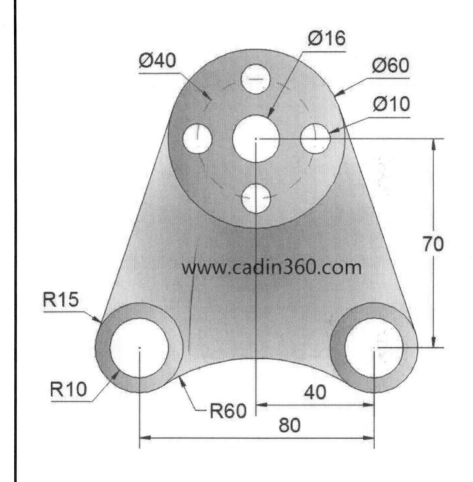

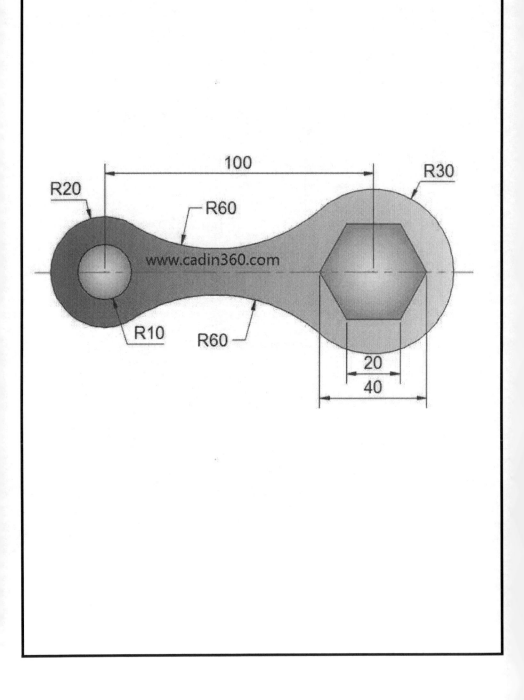

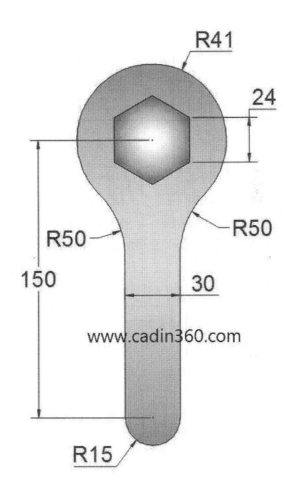

R41

24

R50

R50

150

30

R15

www.cadin360.com

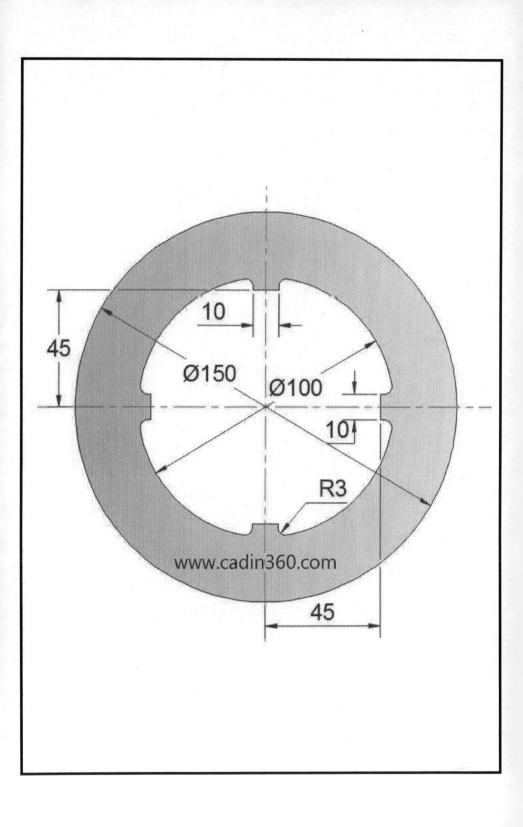

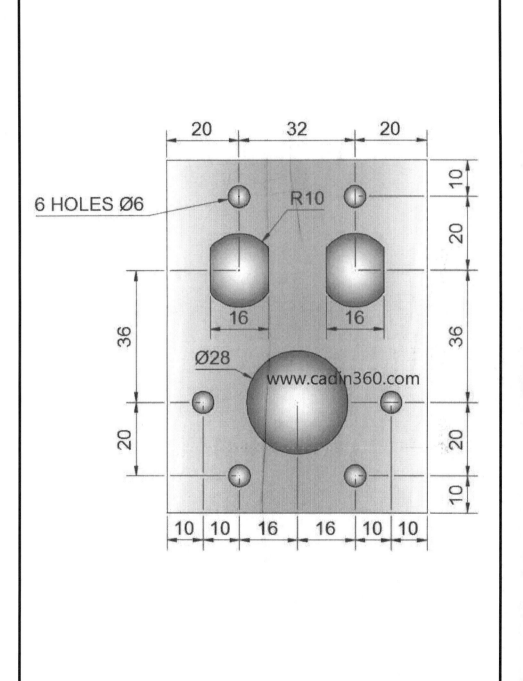

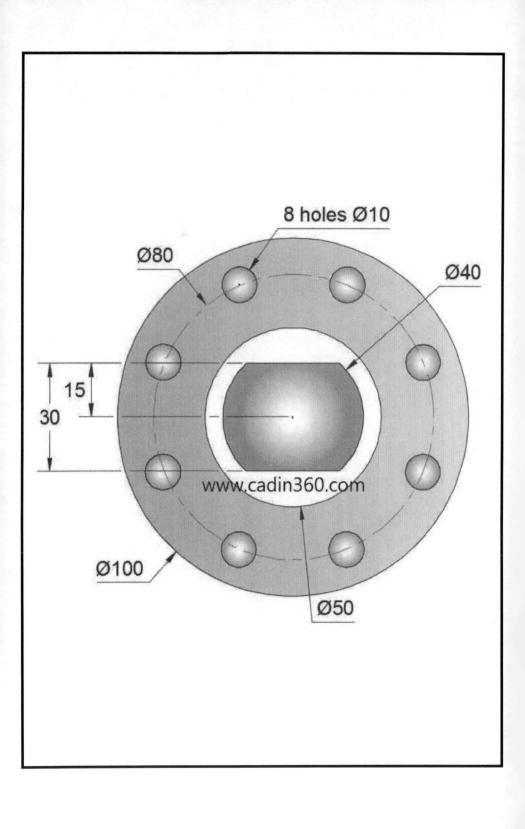

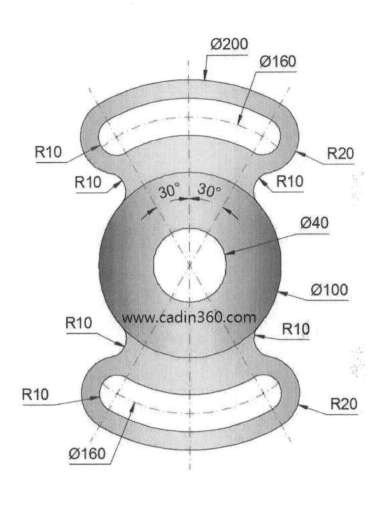

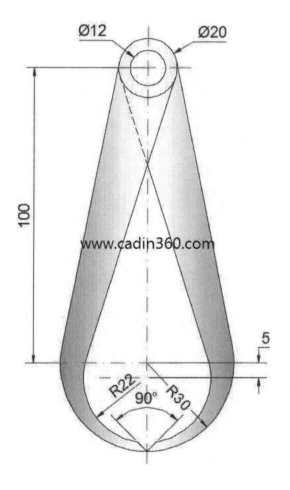

Ø12 Ø20

100

5

R22 90° R30

www.cadin360.com

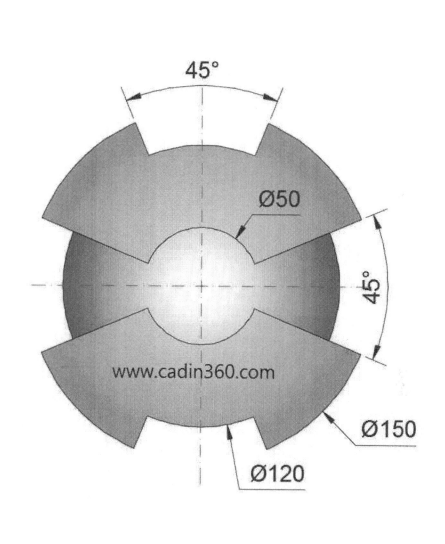

www.cadin360.com

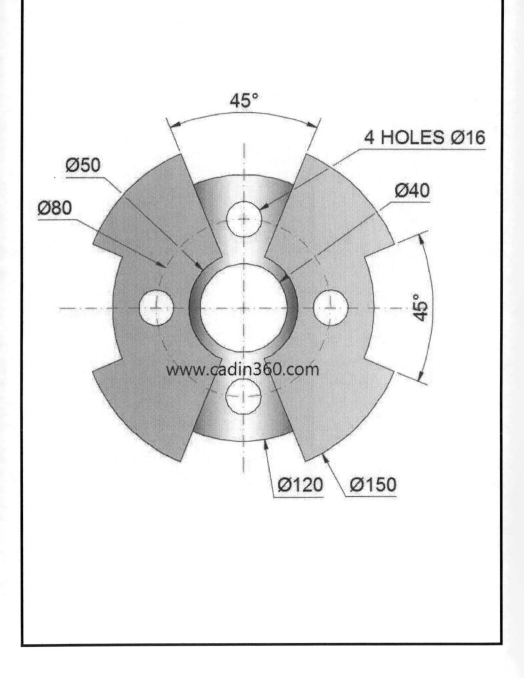

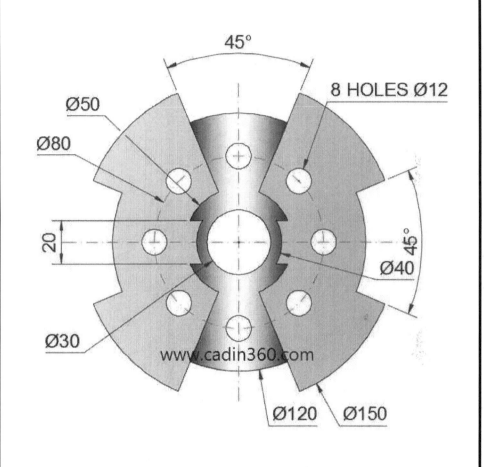

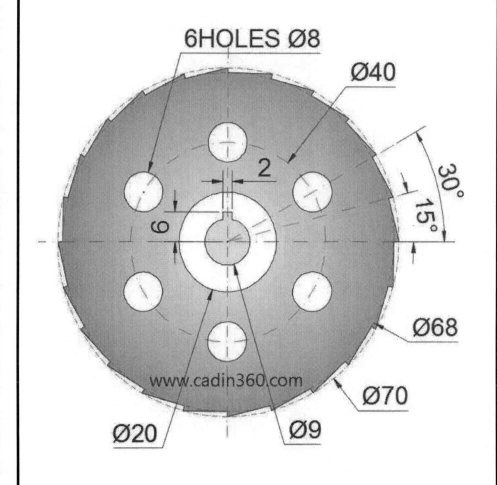

6HOLES Ø8

Ø40

30°

15°

2

9

Ø68

Ø70

Ø20

Ø9

www.cadin360.com

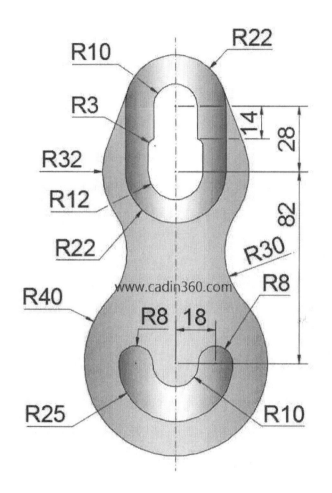

R10　R22

R3

R32

R12

R22

14

28

82

R30

R40

R8

R8　18

R25

R10

www.cadin360.com

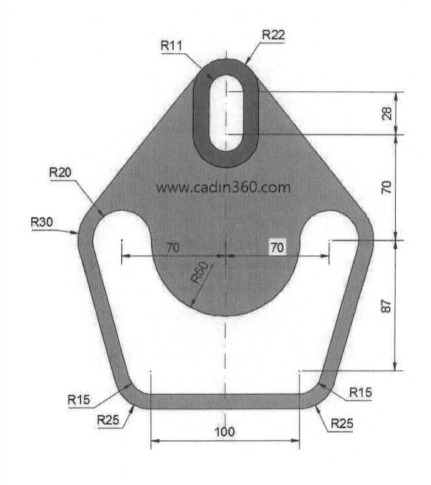

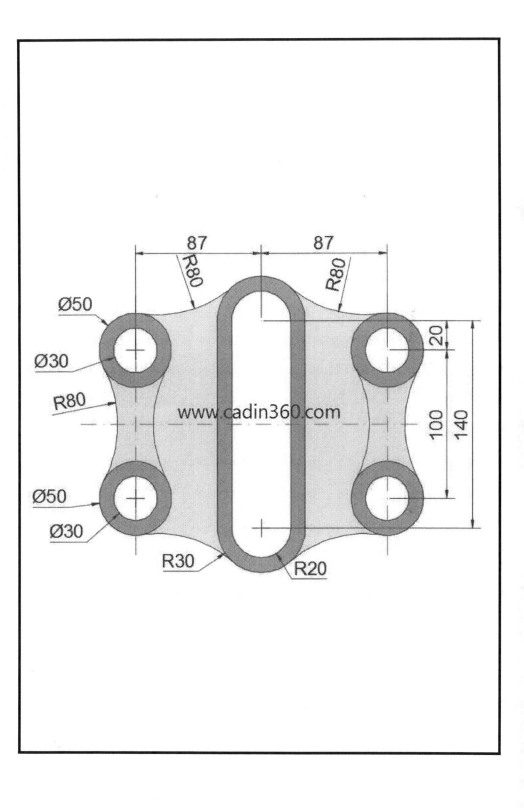

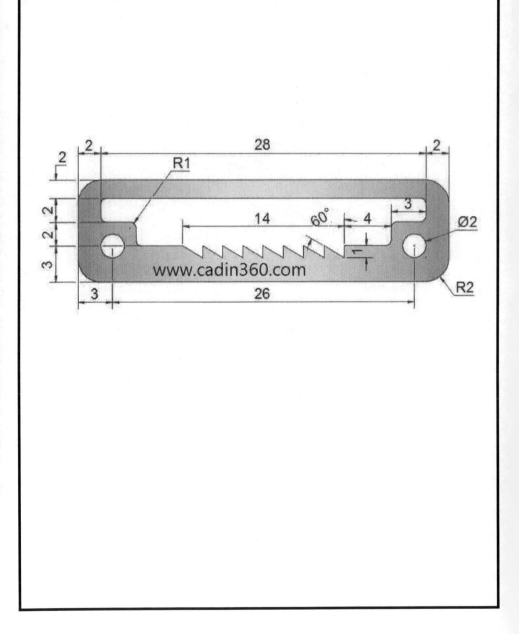

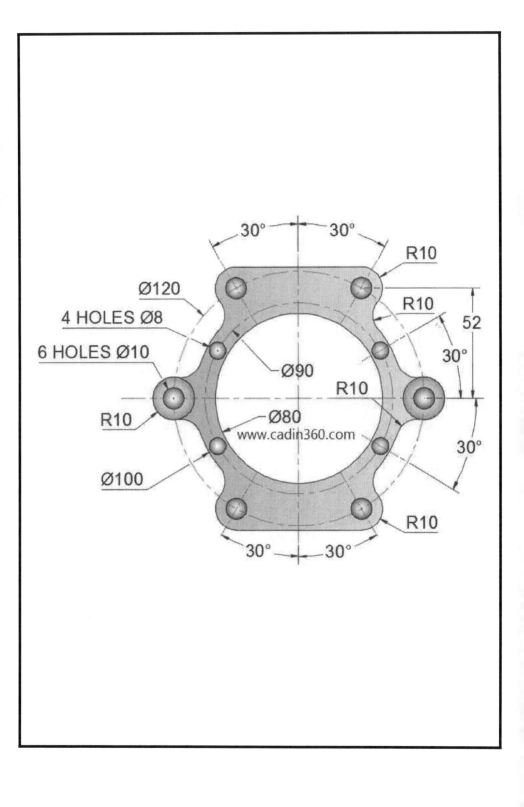

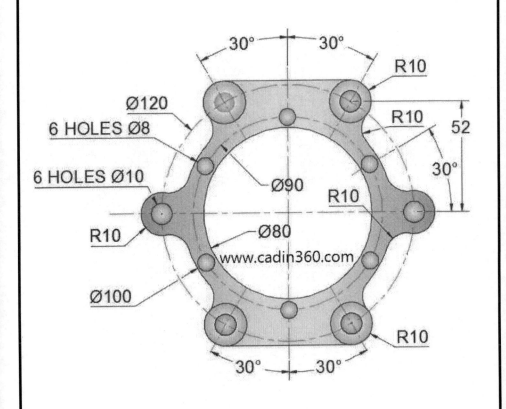

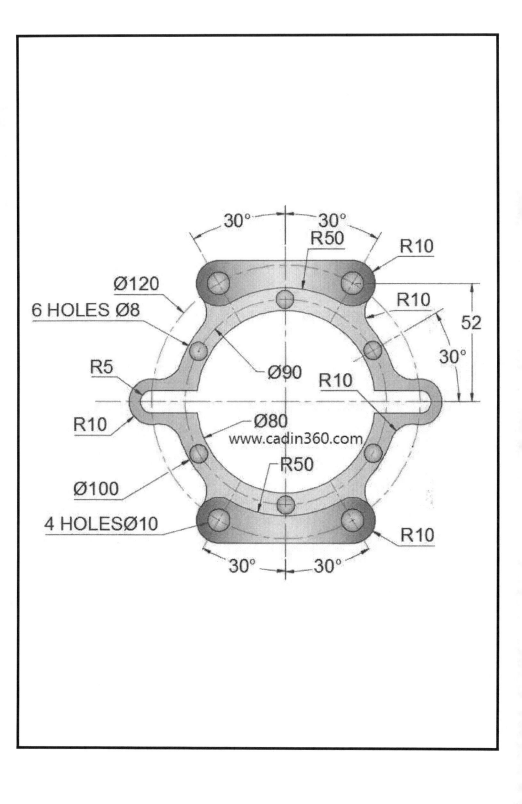

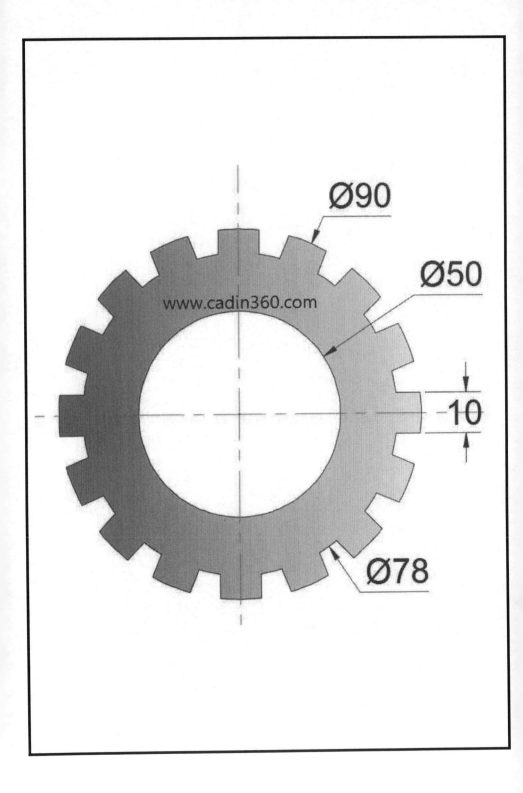

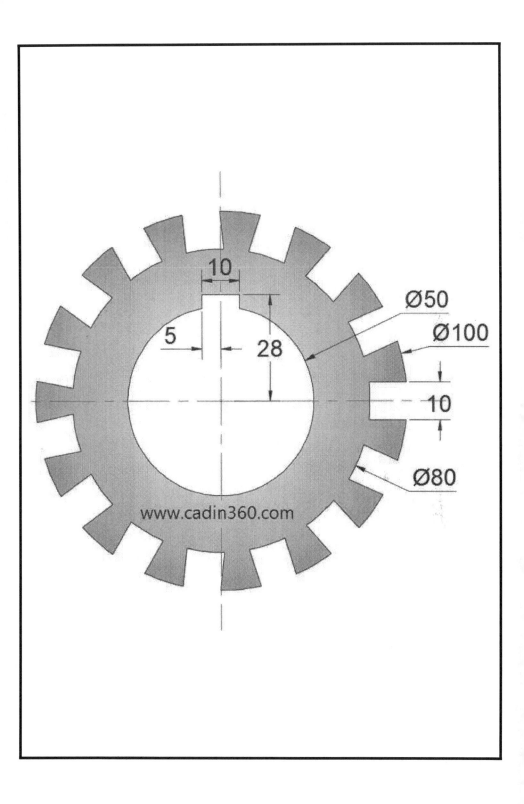
www.cadin360.com

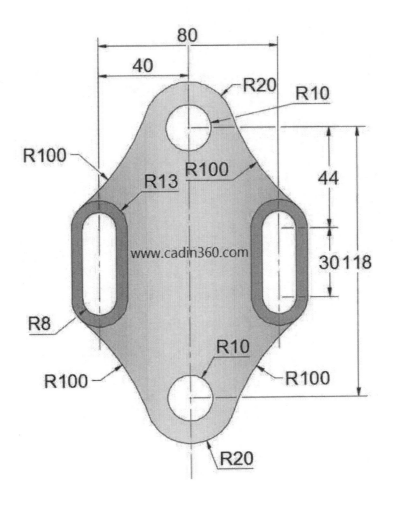

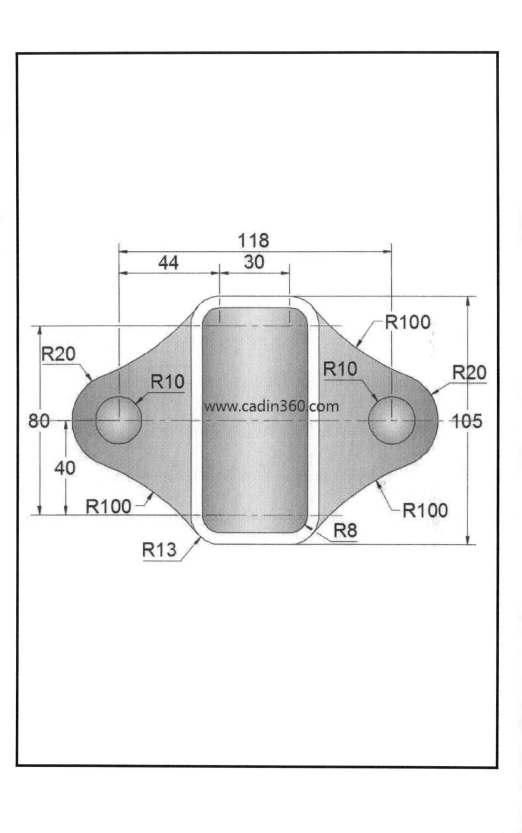

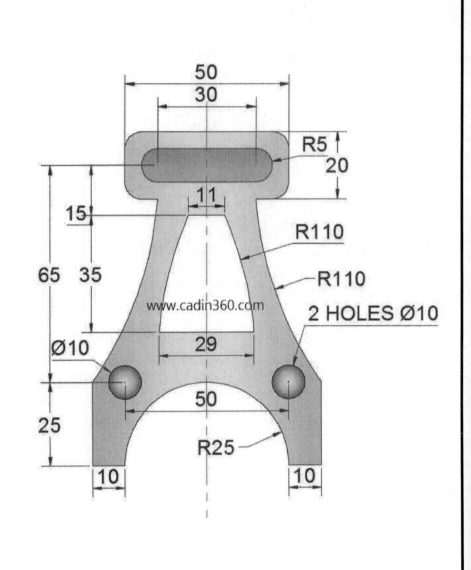

www.cadin360.com

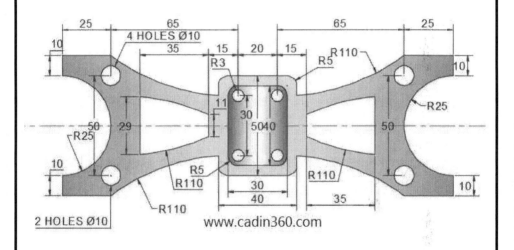

www.cadin360.com

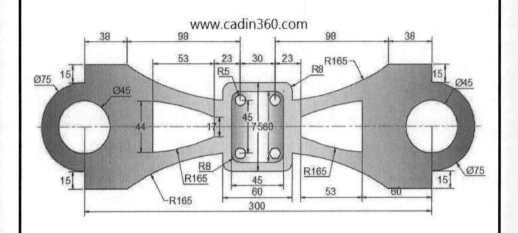
www.cadin360.com

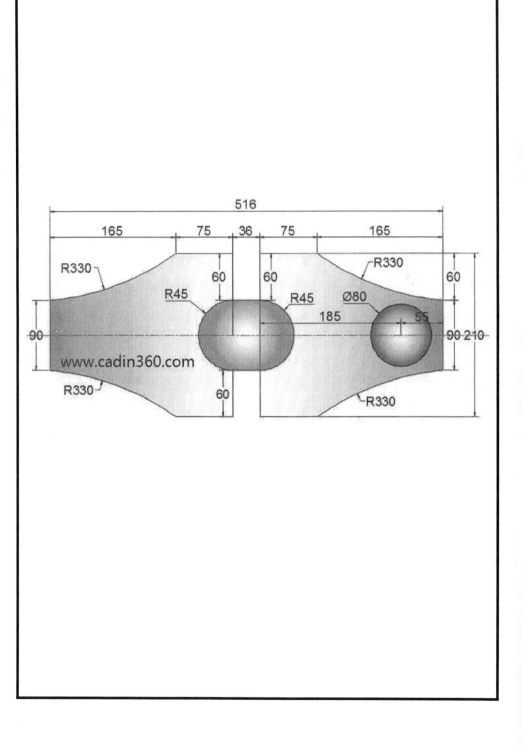

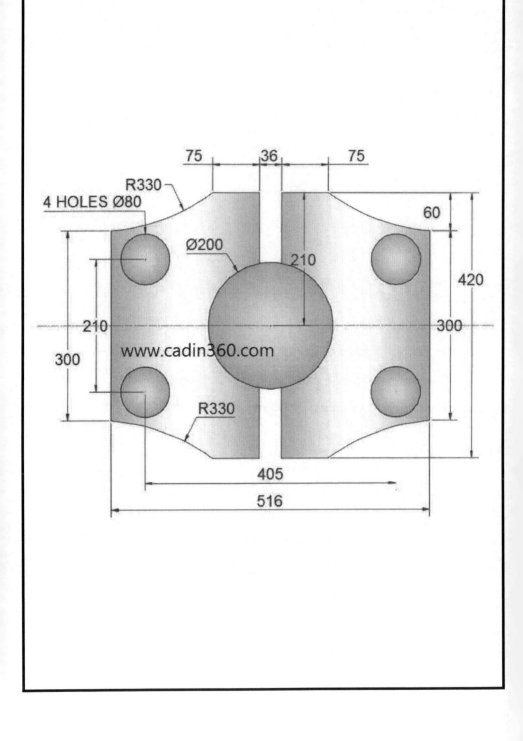

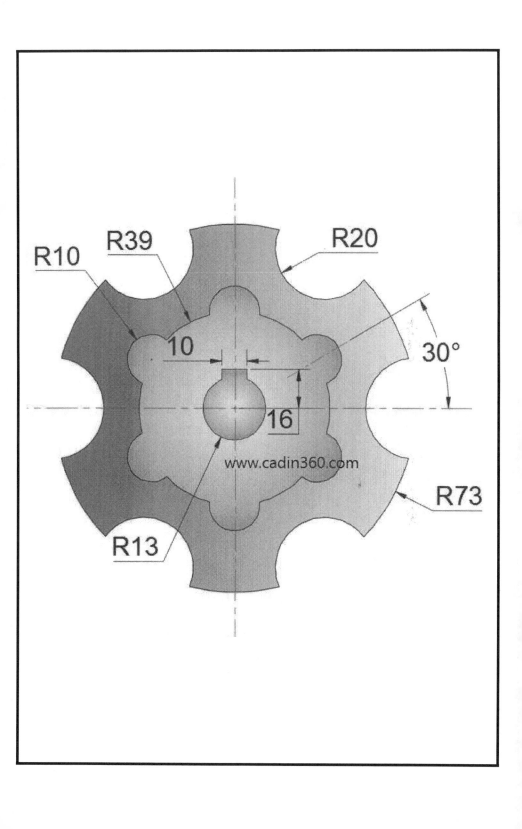

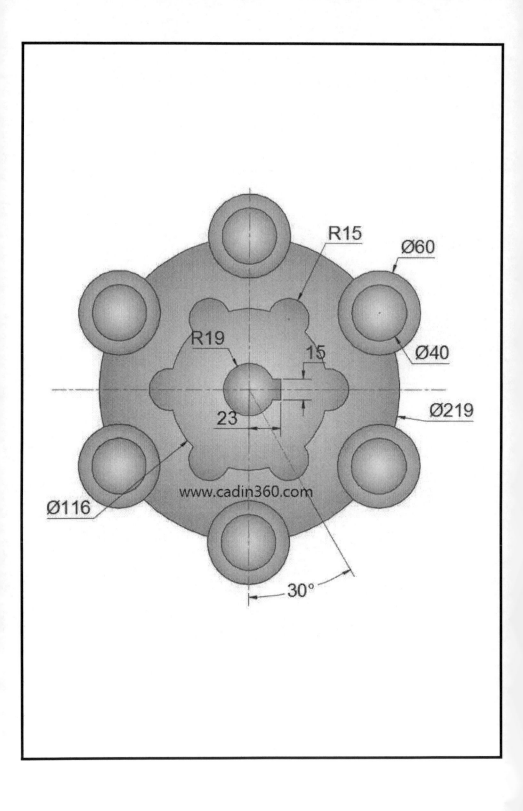

R15

Ø60

Ø40

R19

15

Ø219

23

Ø116

www.cadin360.com

30°

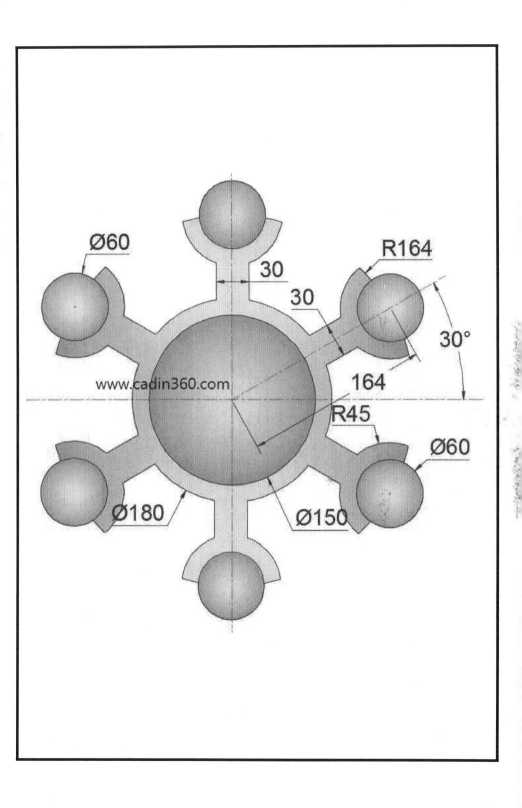

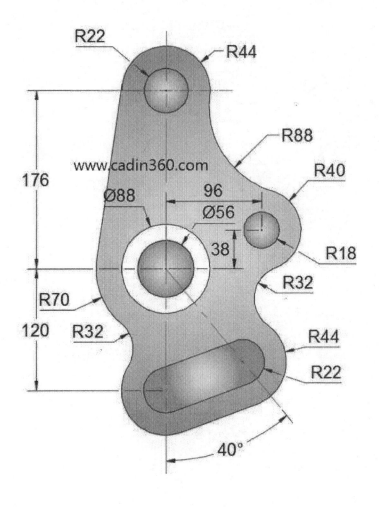

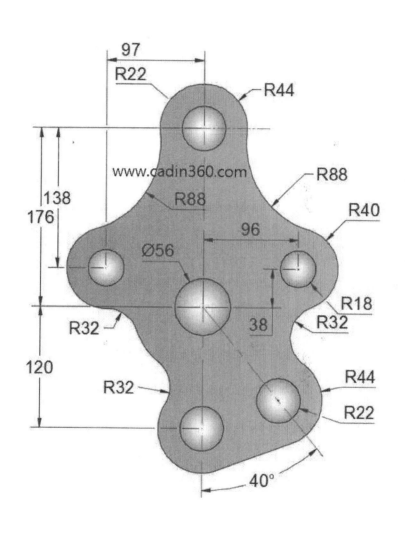

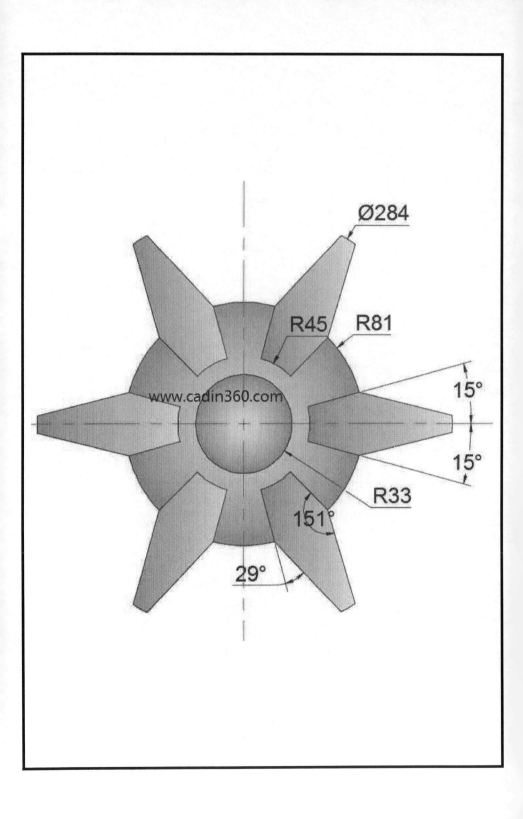

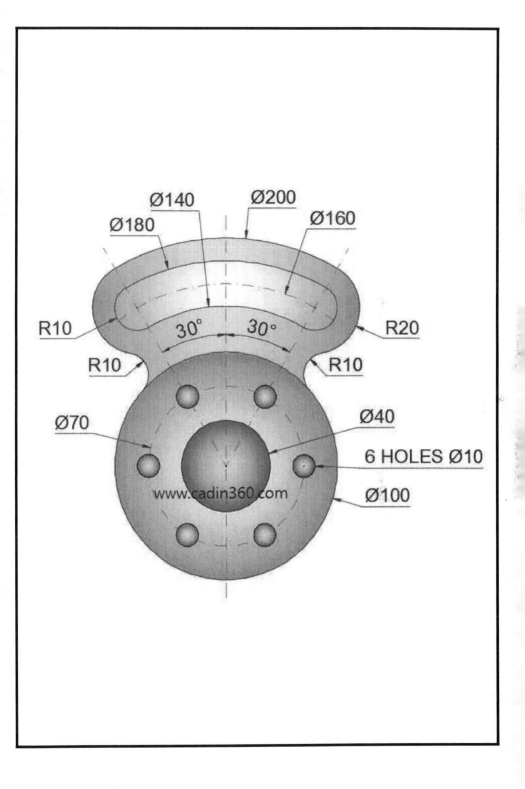

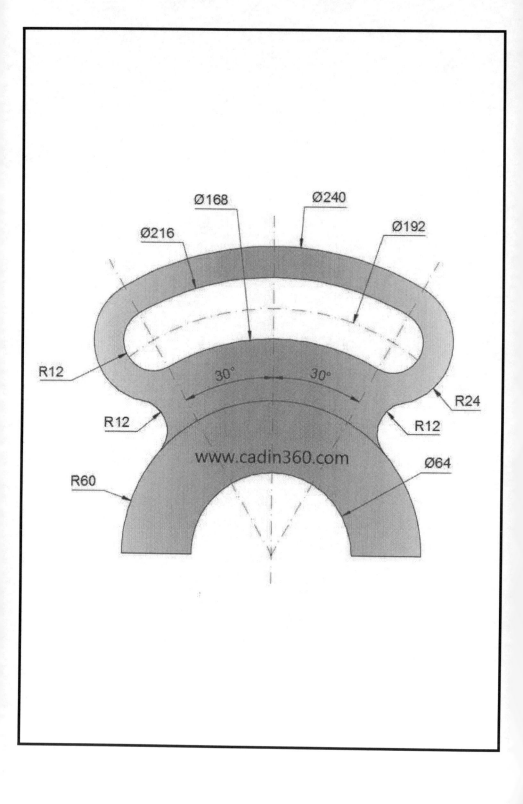

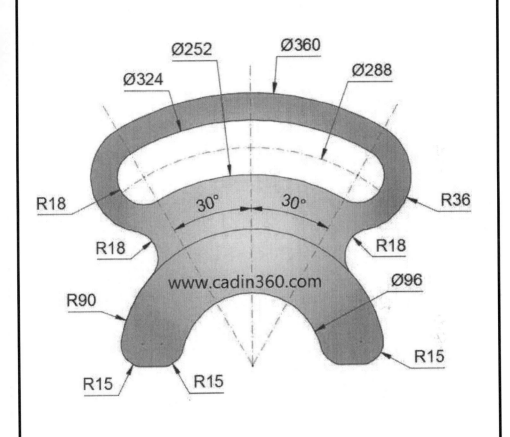

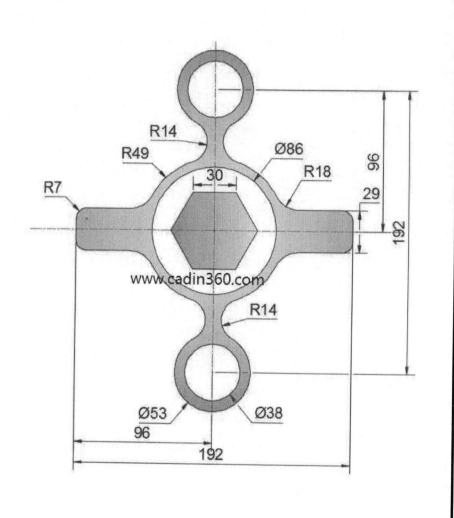

R14
R49
R7
Ø86
R18
30
96
29
192
R14
Ø53
96
Ø38
192

www.cadin360.com

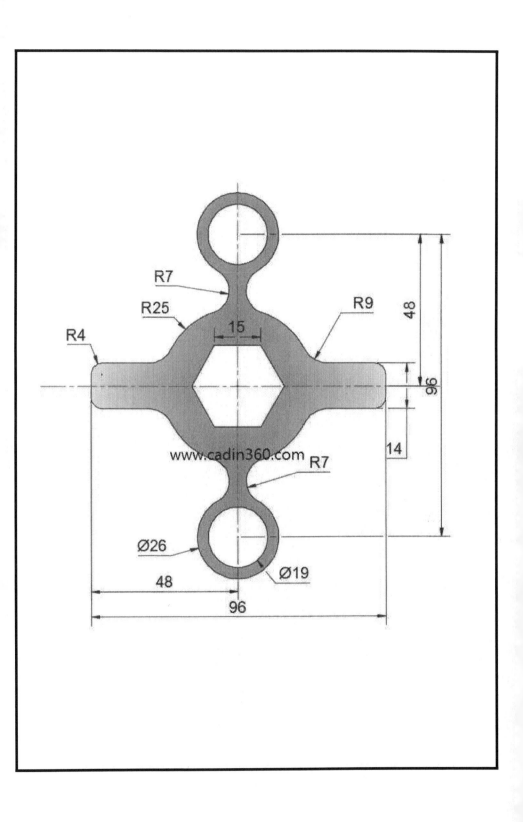

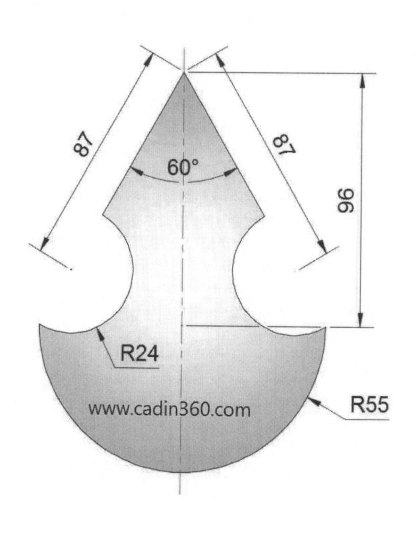

87 87 60° 96 R24 www.cadin360.com R55

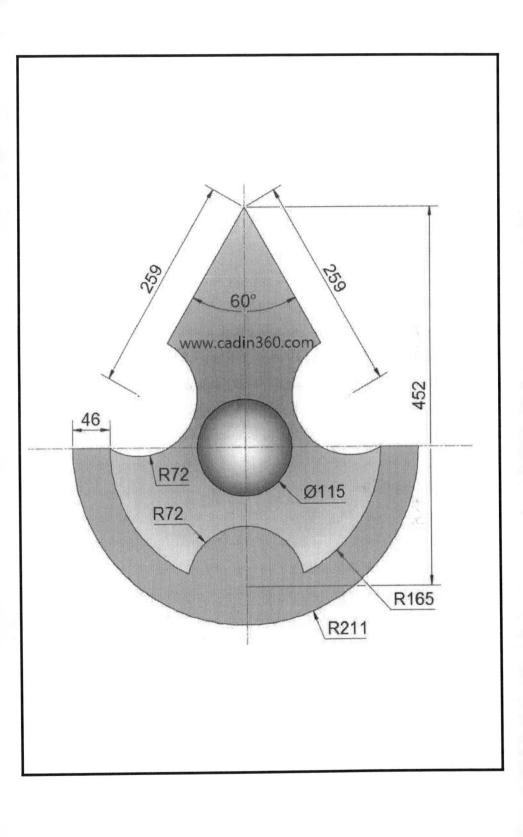

259

259

60°

www.cadin360.com

452

46

R72

R72

Ø115

R165

R211

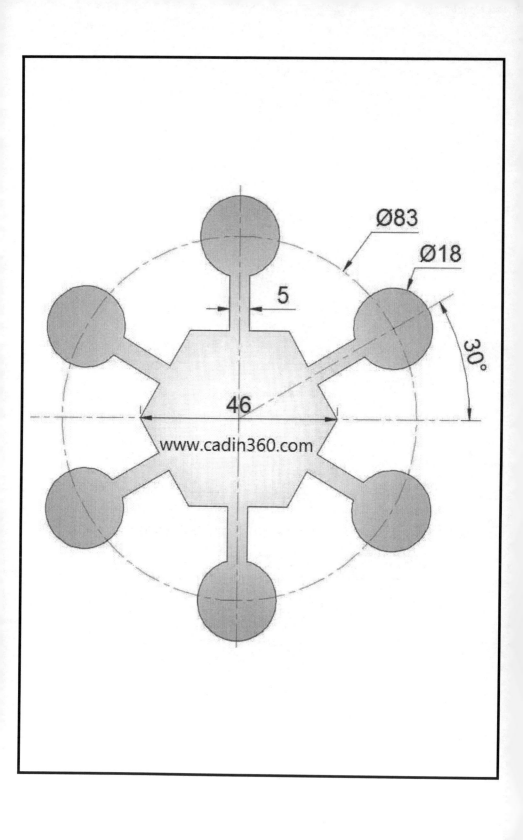

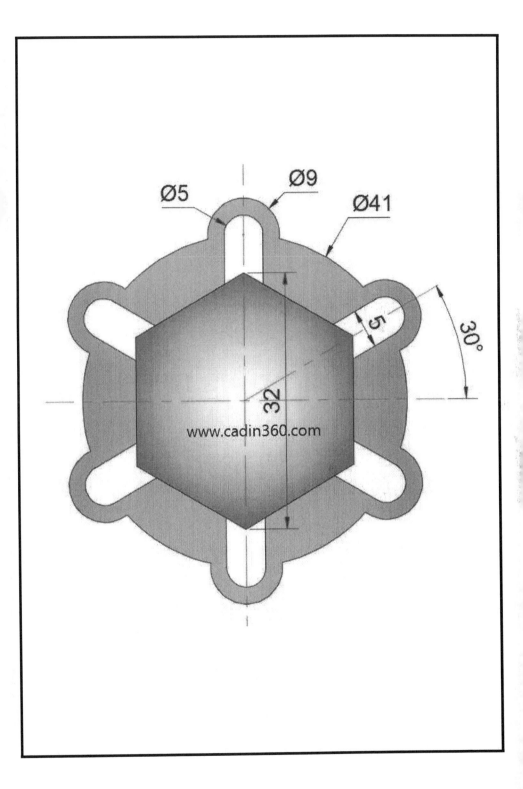

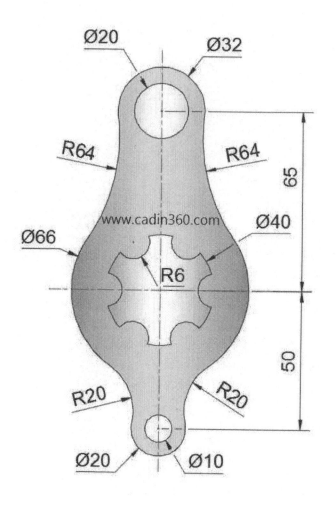

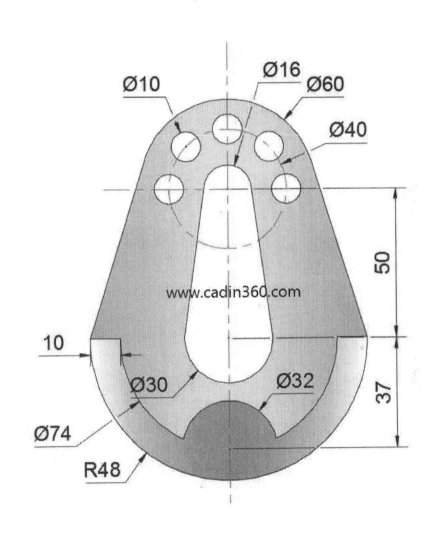

Ø10 Ø16 Ø60 Ø40

www.cadin360.com

10

Ø30 Ø32

Ø74

R48

50

37

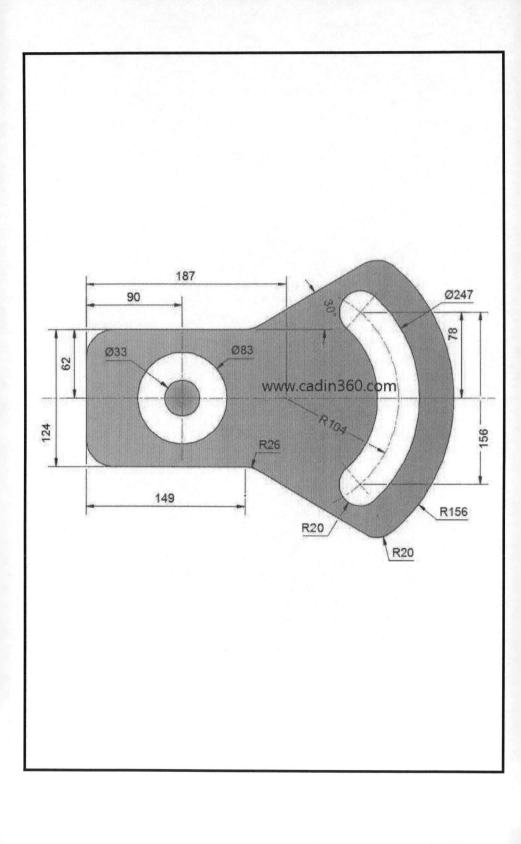

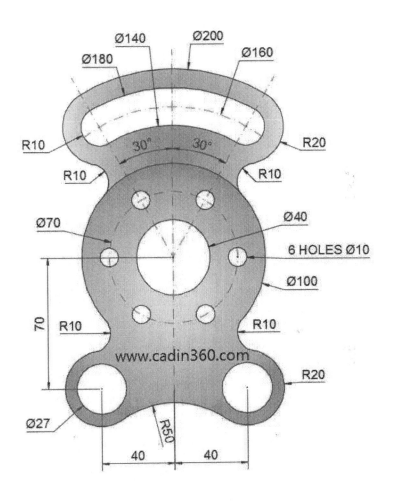

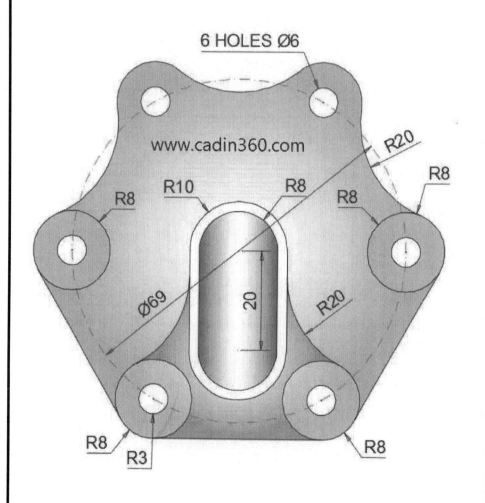

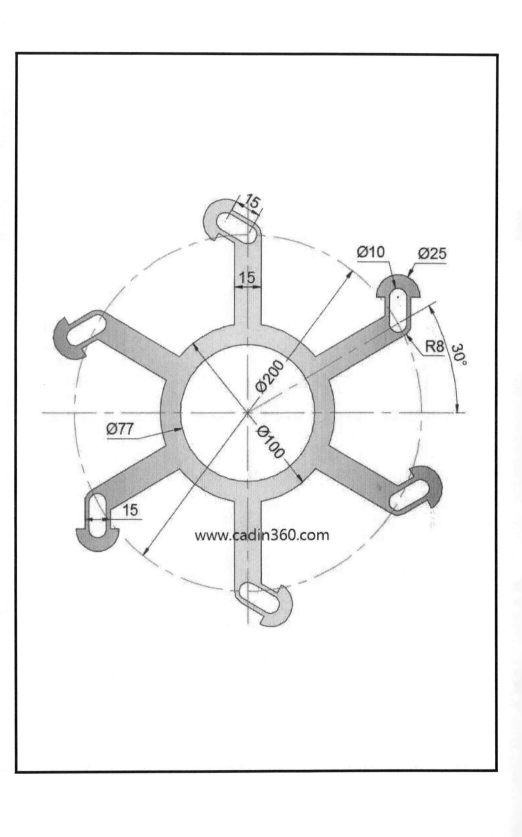

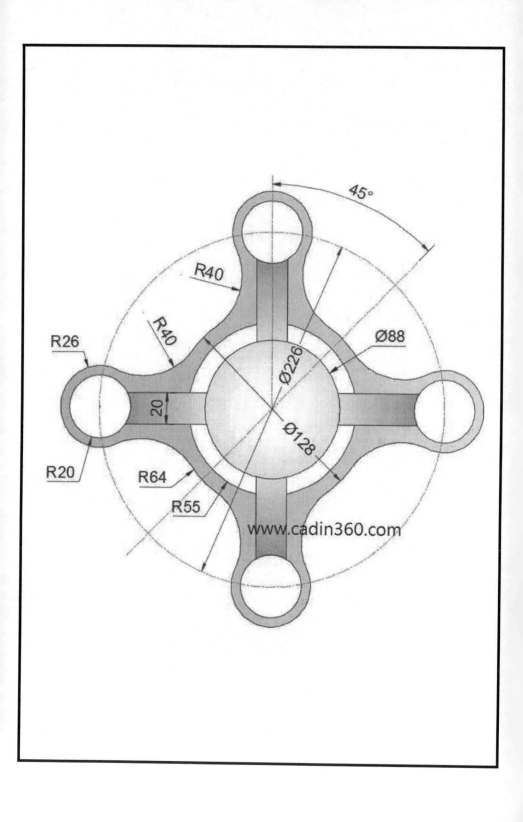

45°

R40

R40

R26

R20

R64

R55

20

Ø226

Ø128

Ø88

www.cadin360.com

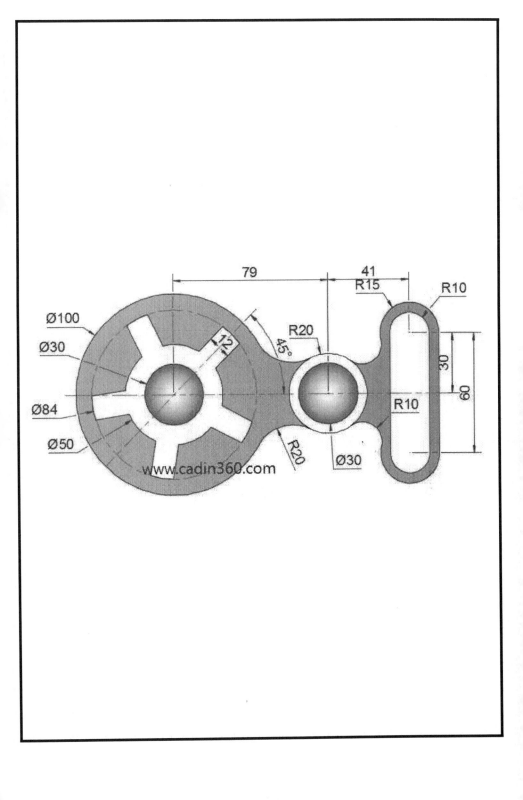

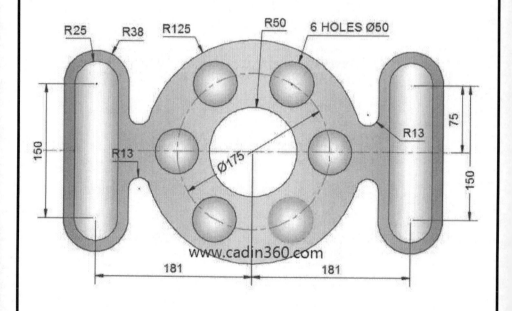

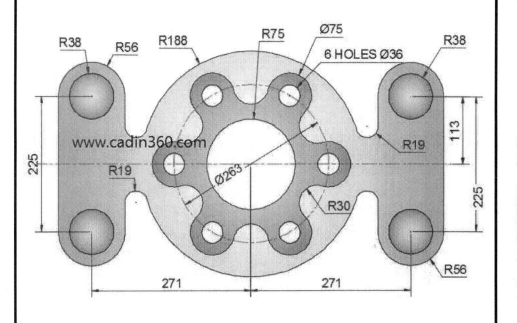

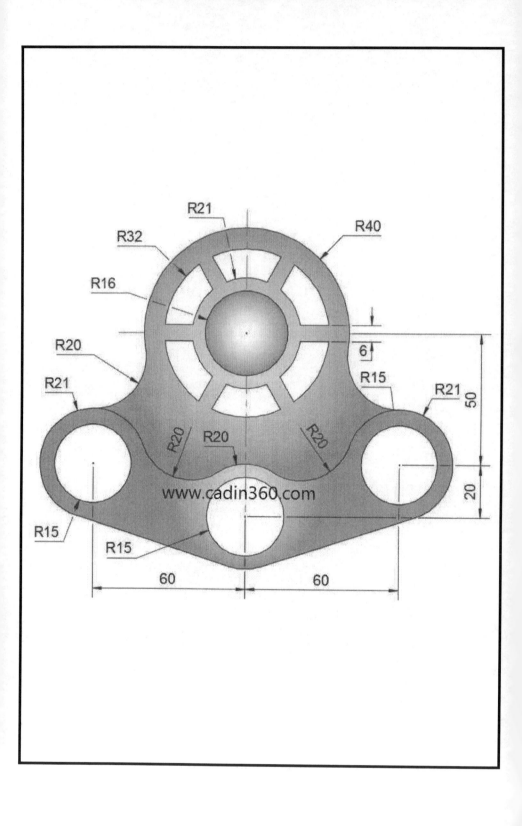

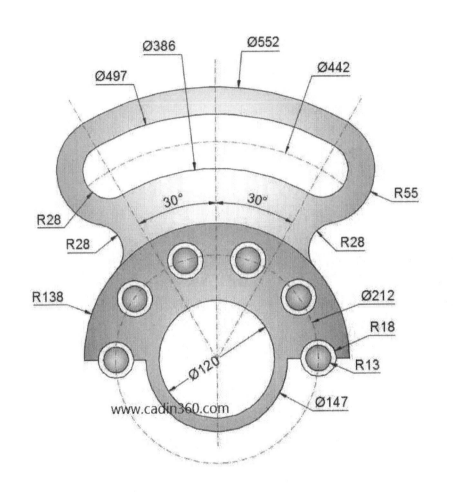

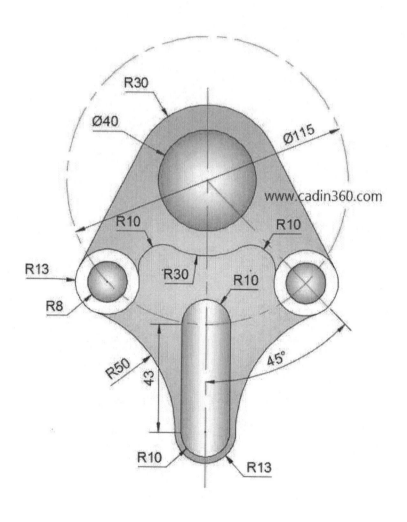

R30

Ø40

R30

Ø115

www.cadin360.com

R10

R10

R13

R30

R10

R8

R50

R10

43

45°

R10

R13

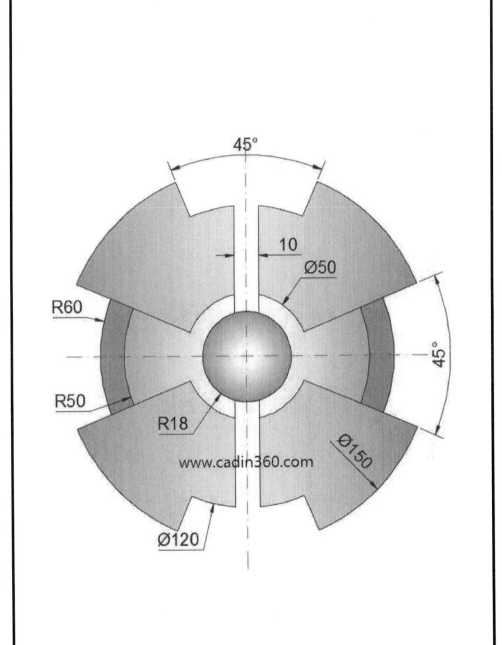
www.cadin360.com

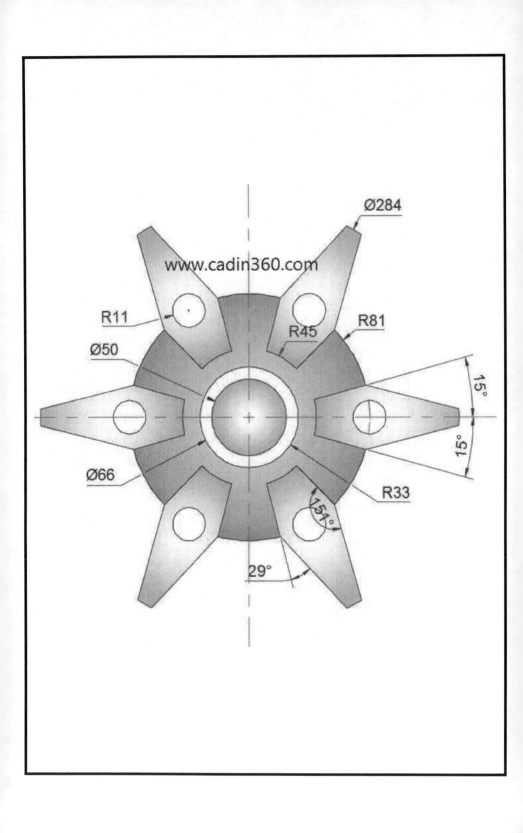

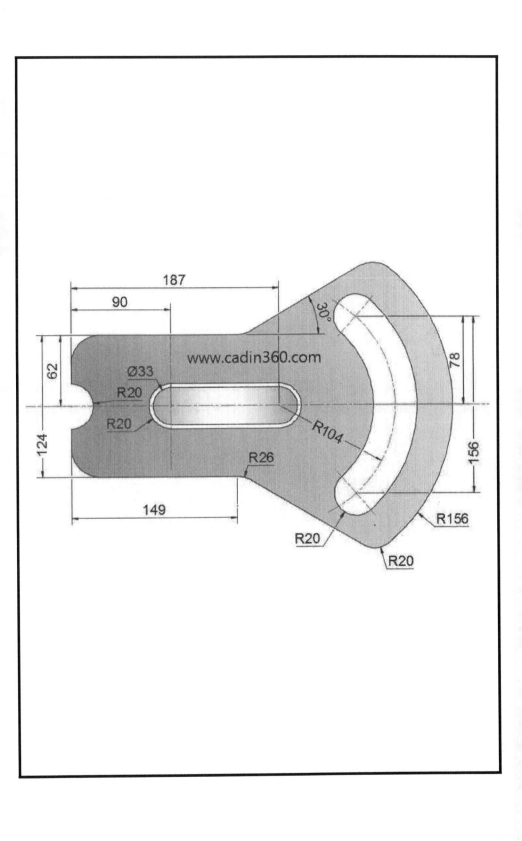

3D EXERCISES

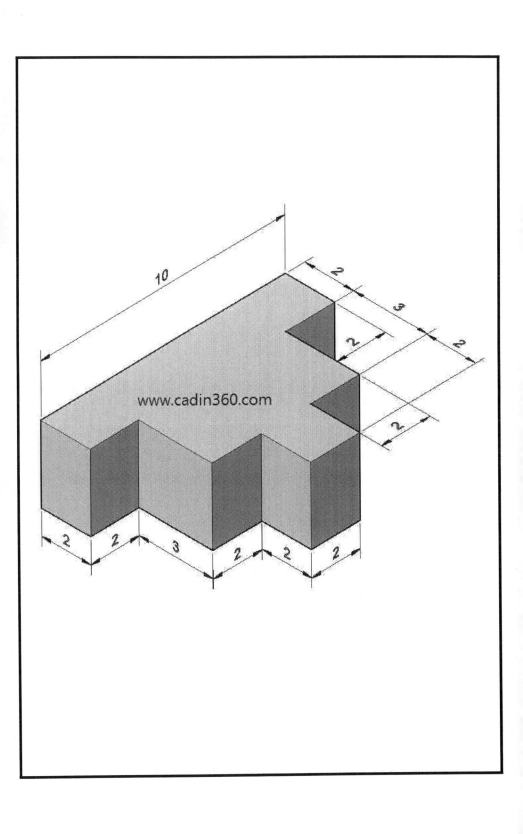

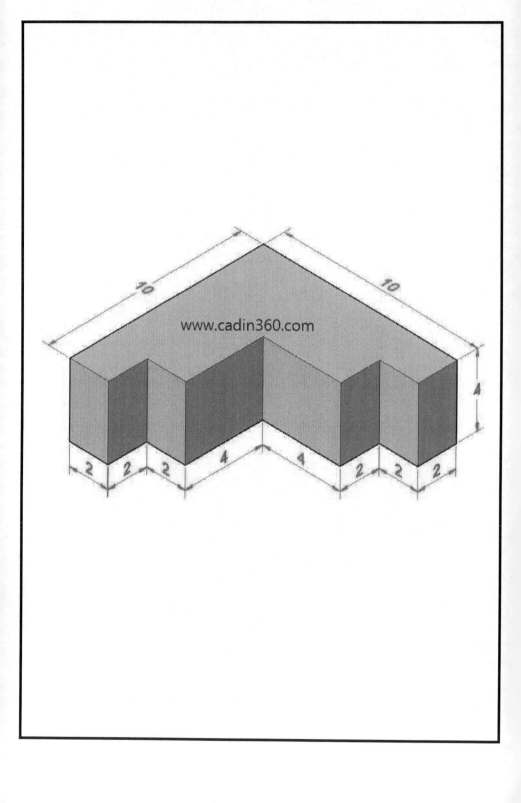

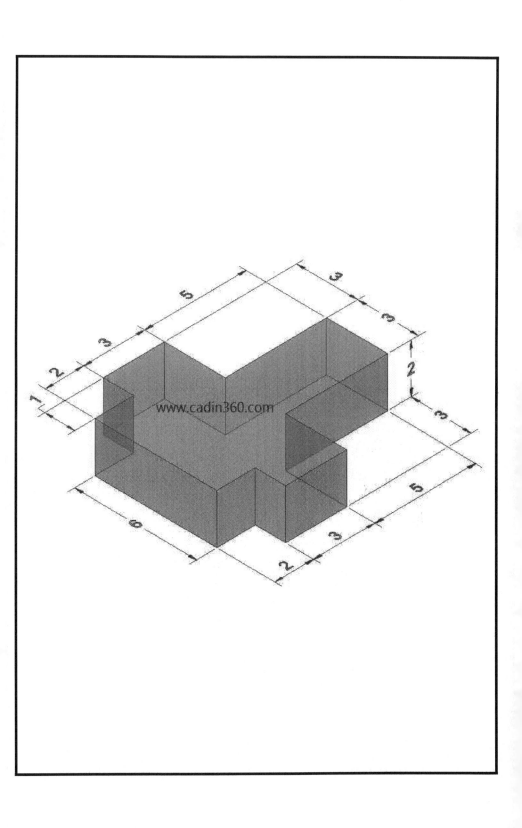

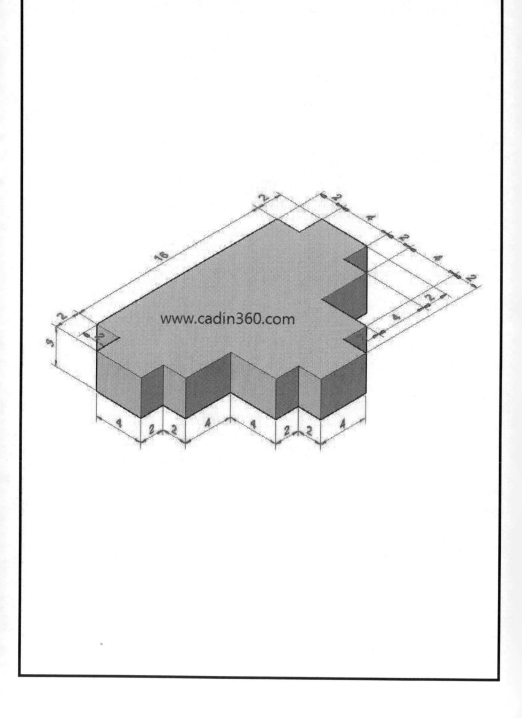
www.cadin360.com

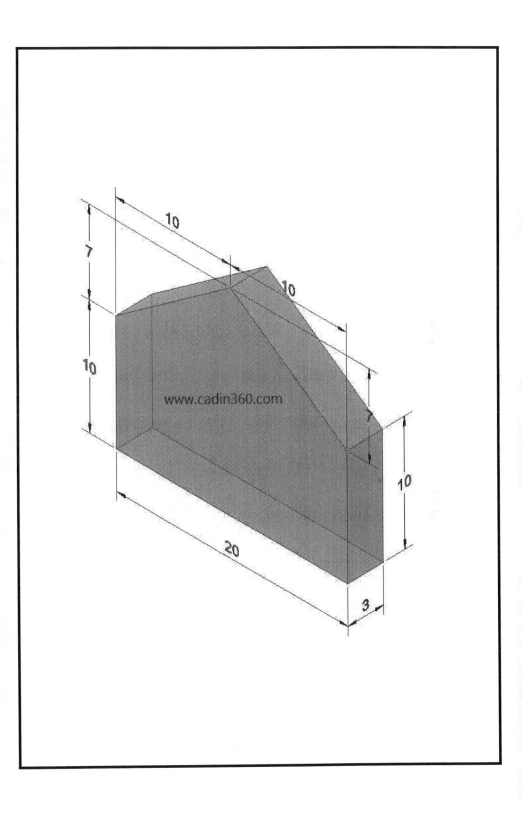

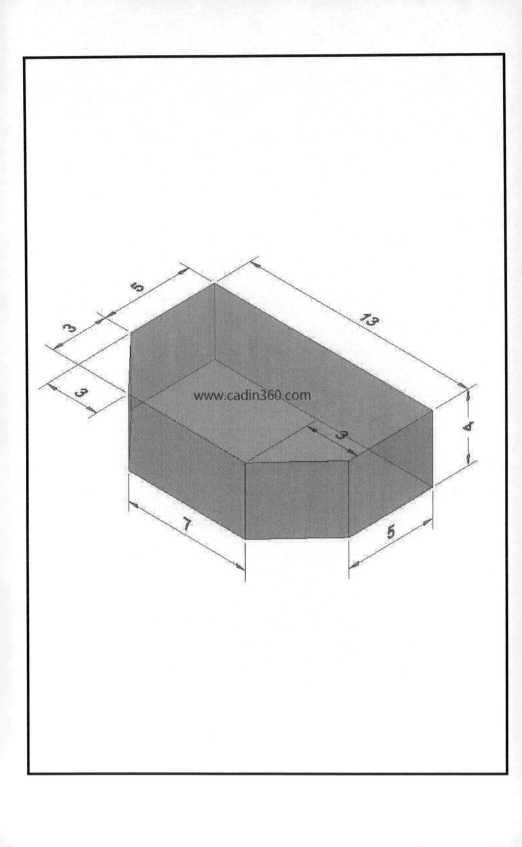

www.cadin360.com

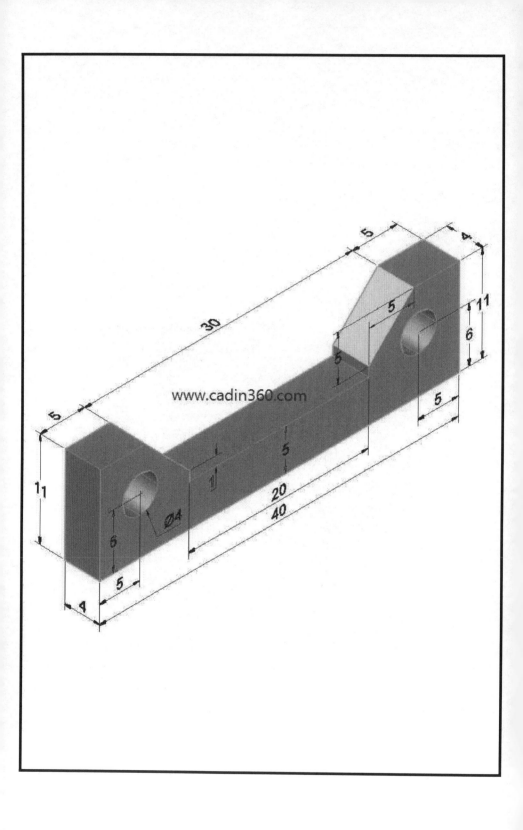

www.cadin360.com

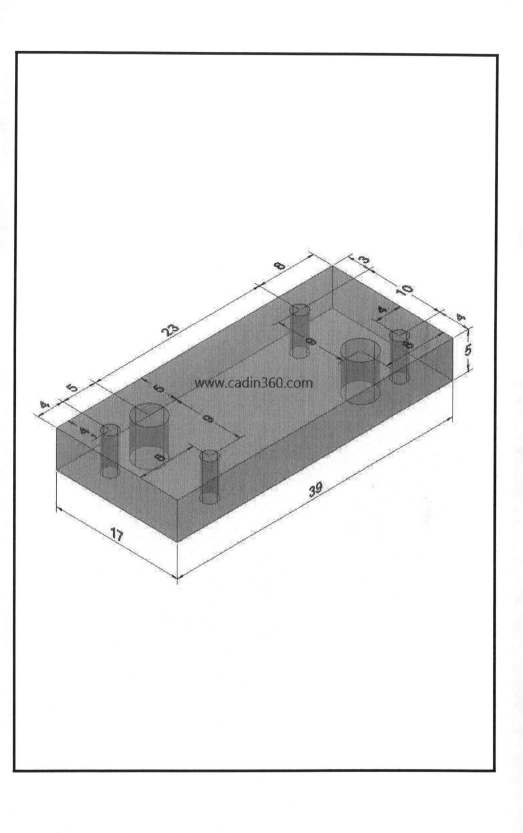

www.cadin360.com

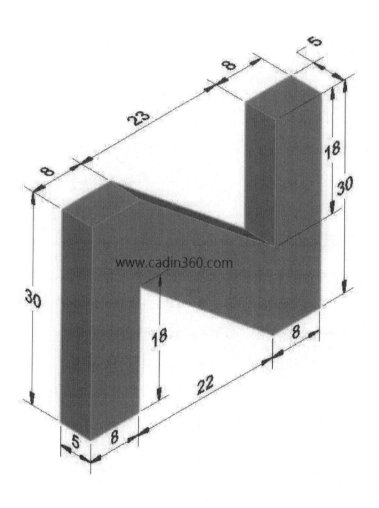

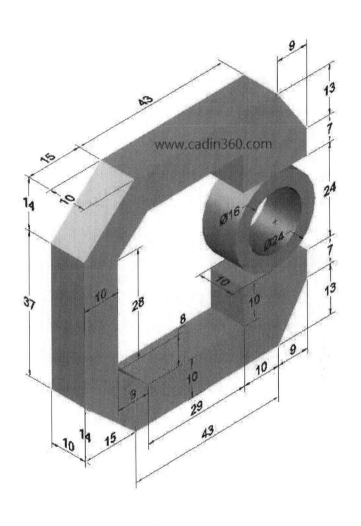

www.cadin360.com

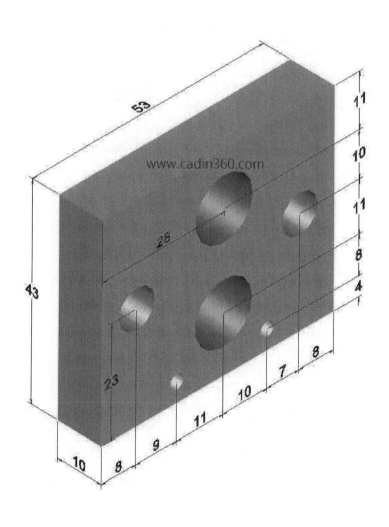

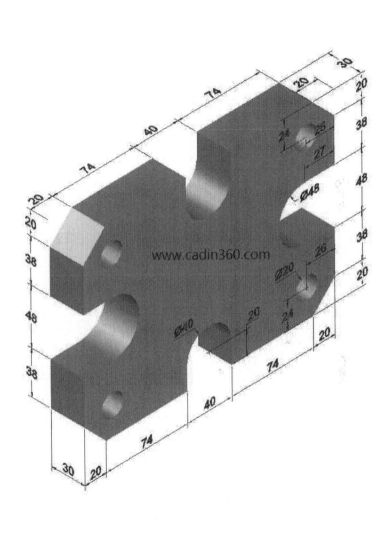

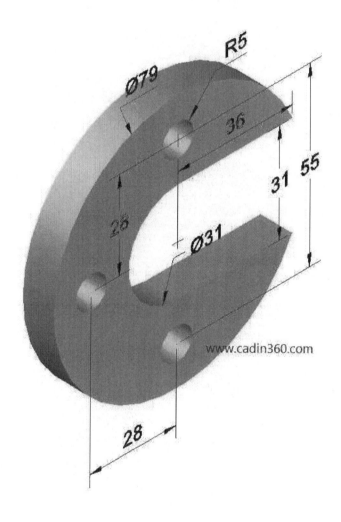

www.cadin360.com

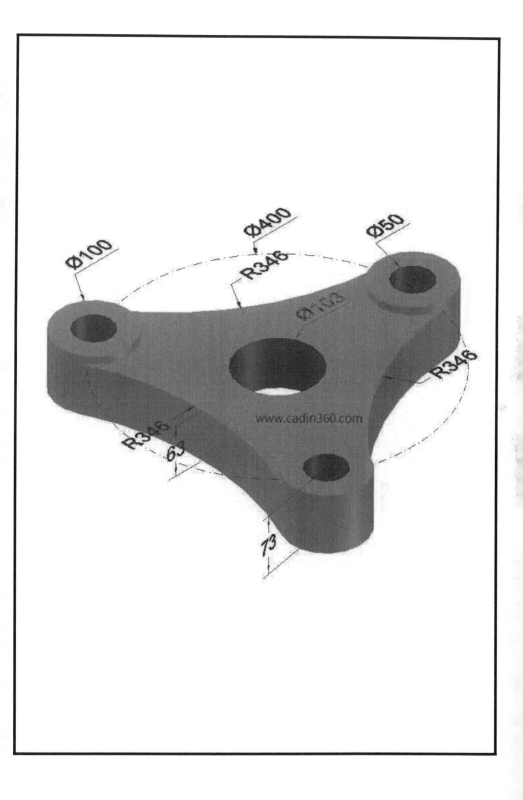

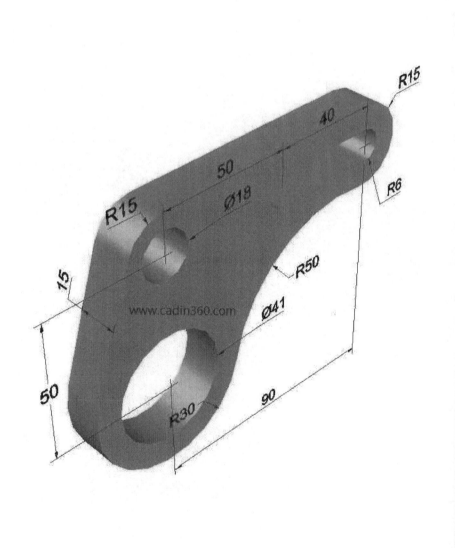

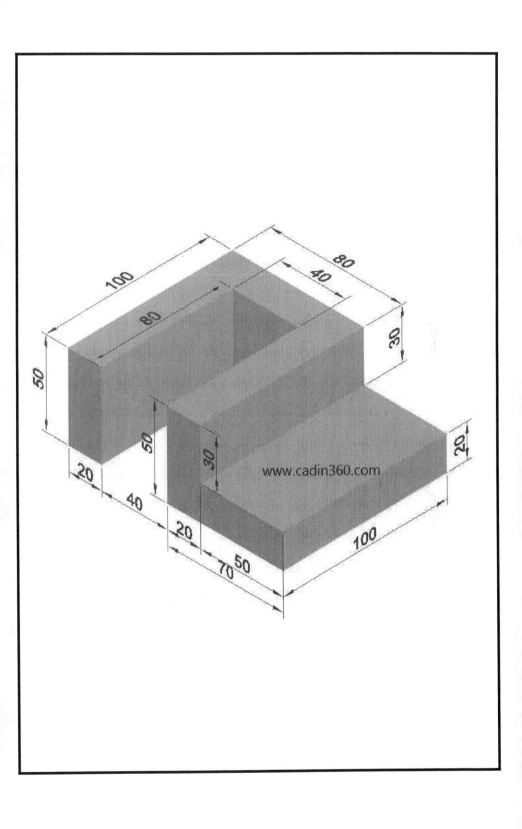

www.cadin360.com

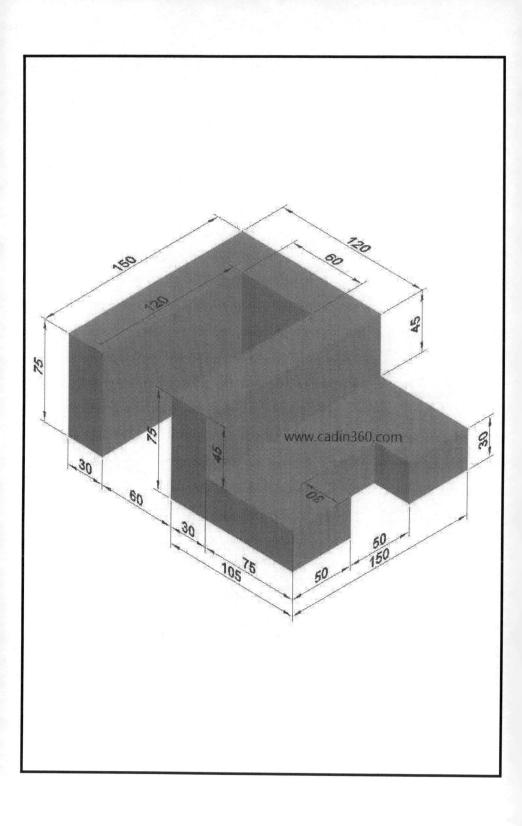

150
120
60
120
45
75
75
45
30
30
60
30
30
50
50
75
105
150

www.cadin360.com

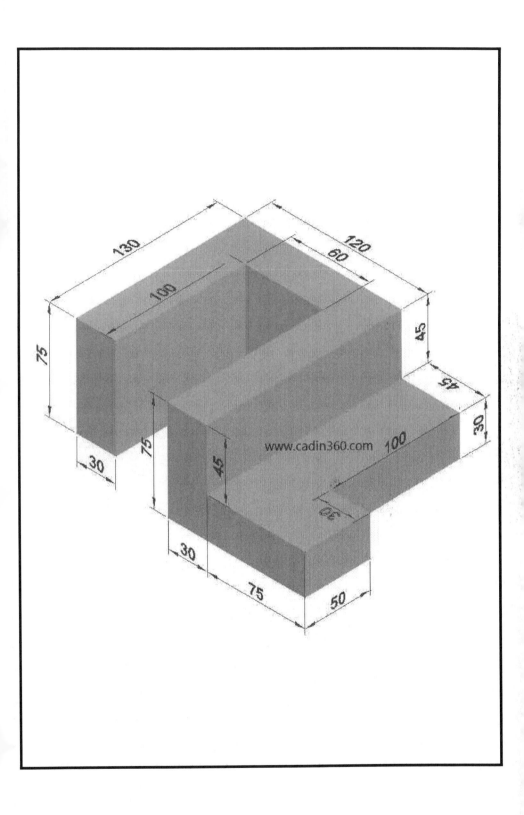

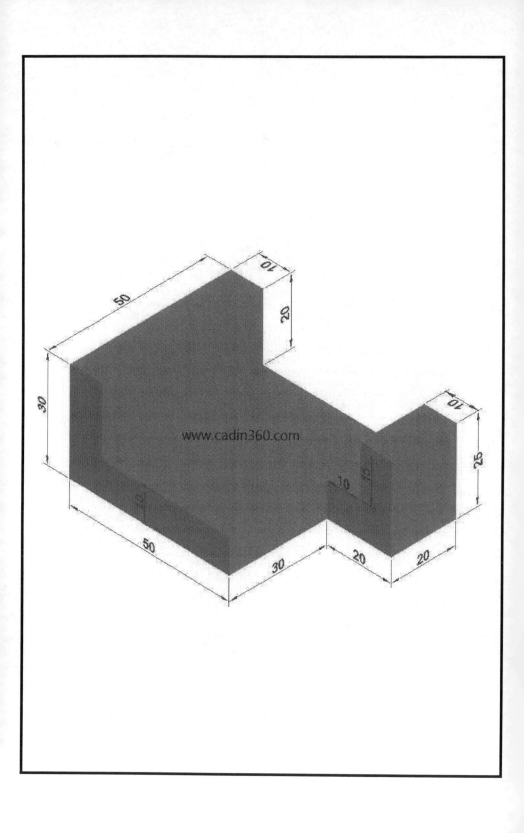

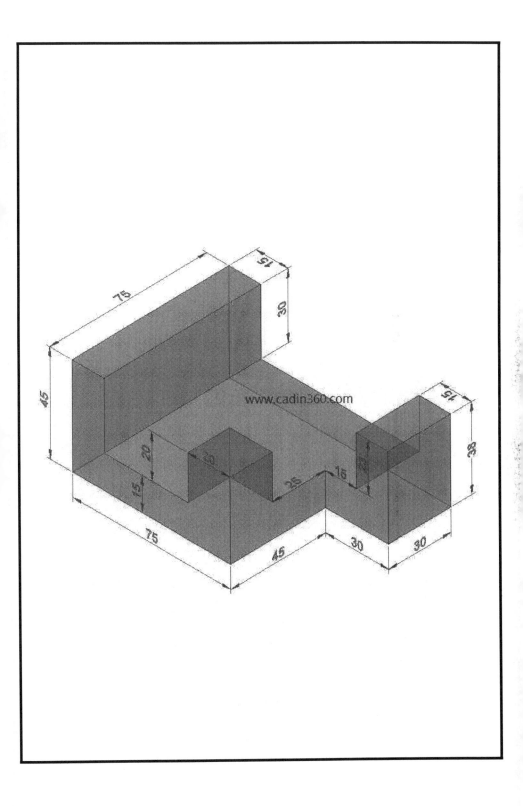

75 · 15 · 30 · 45 · 20 · 20 · 15 · 38 · 15 · 75 · 45 · 30 · 30 · 25

www.cadin360.com

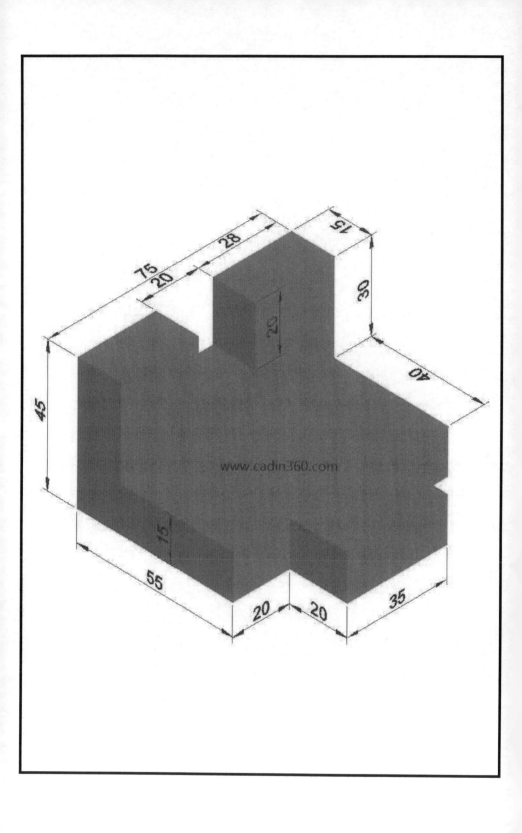

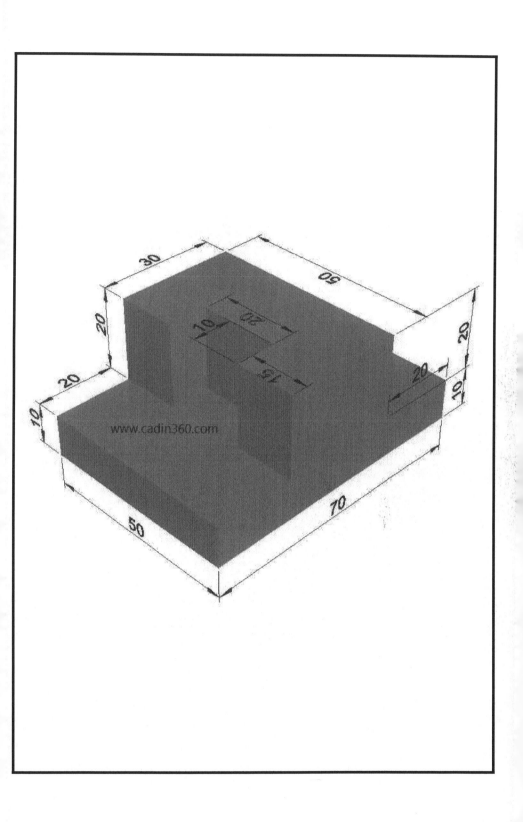

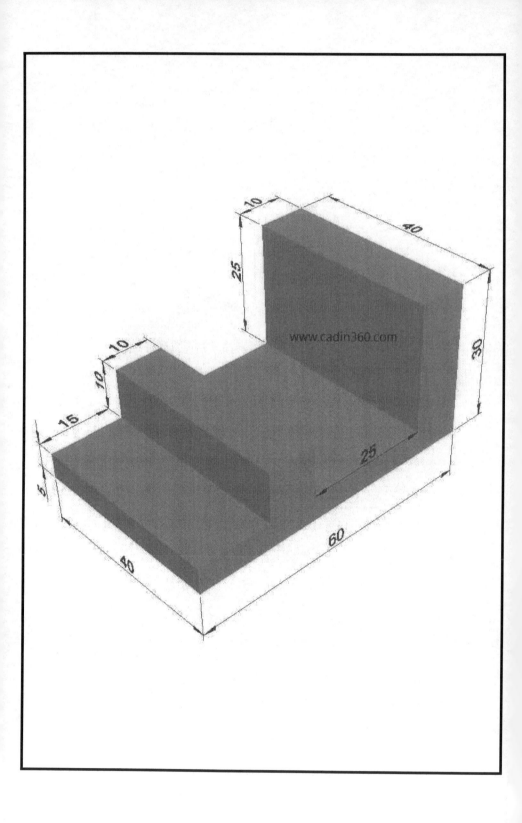

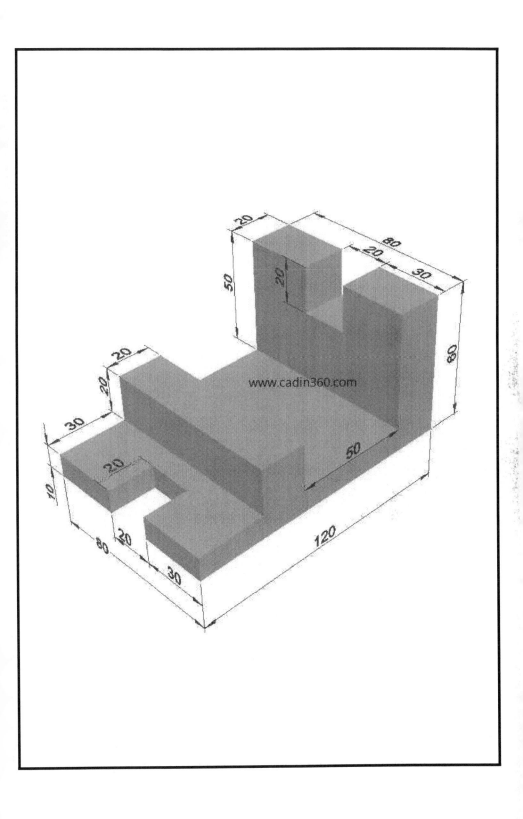

www.cadin360.com

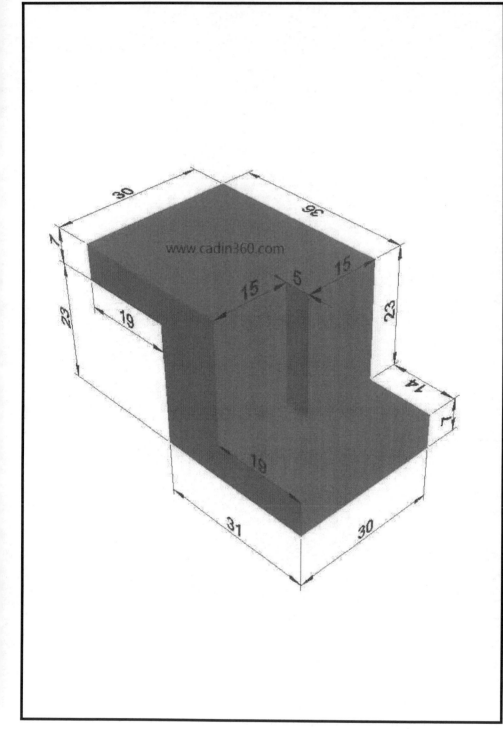

www.cadin360.com

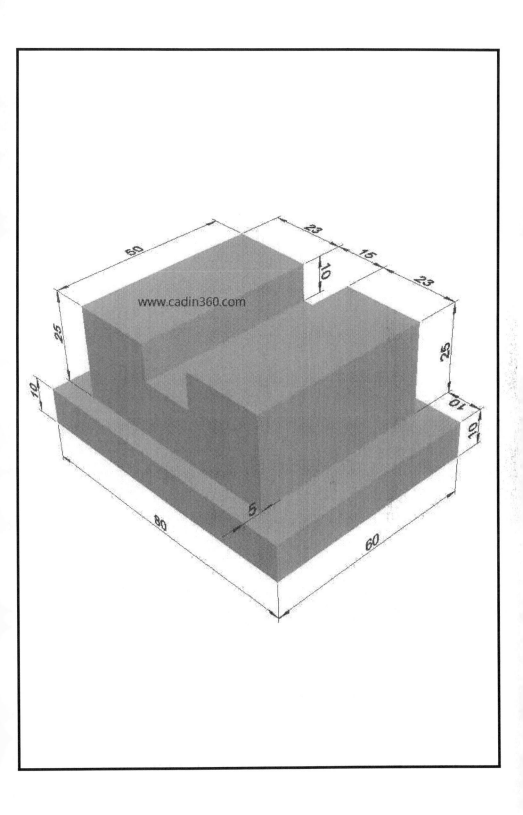
www.cadin360.com

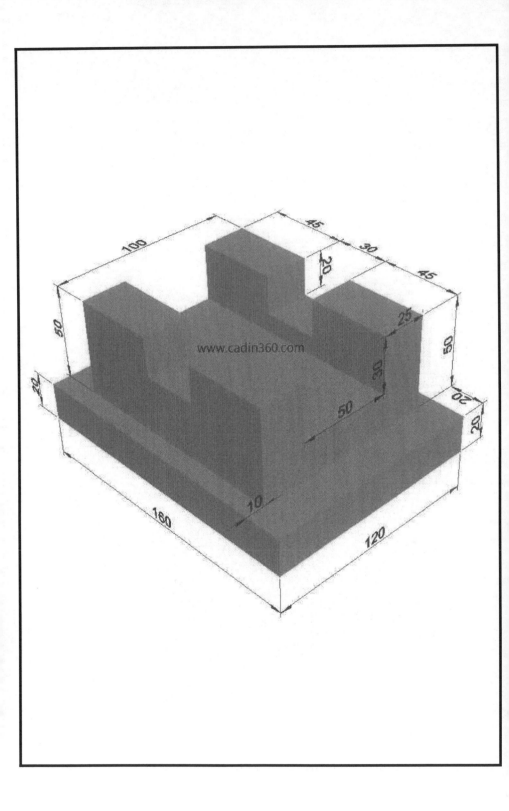

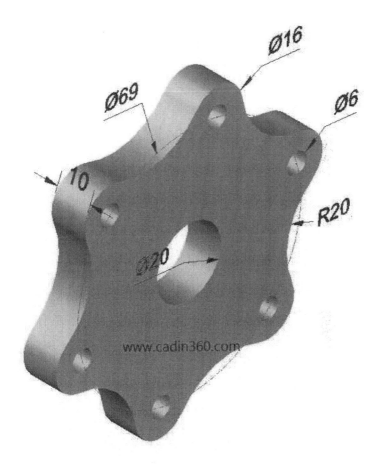

Ø16

Ø69

Ø6

10

R20

Ø20

www.cadin360.com

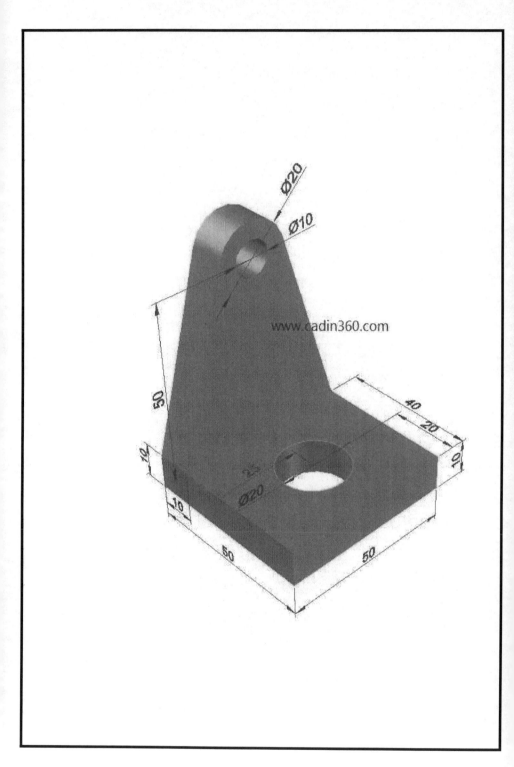

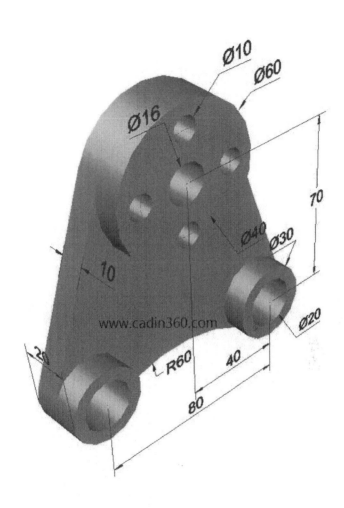

Ø10

Ø60

Ø16

70

10

Ø40

Ø30

Ø20

20

R60

40

www.cadin360.com

80

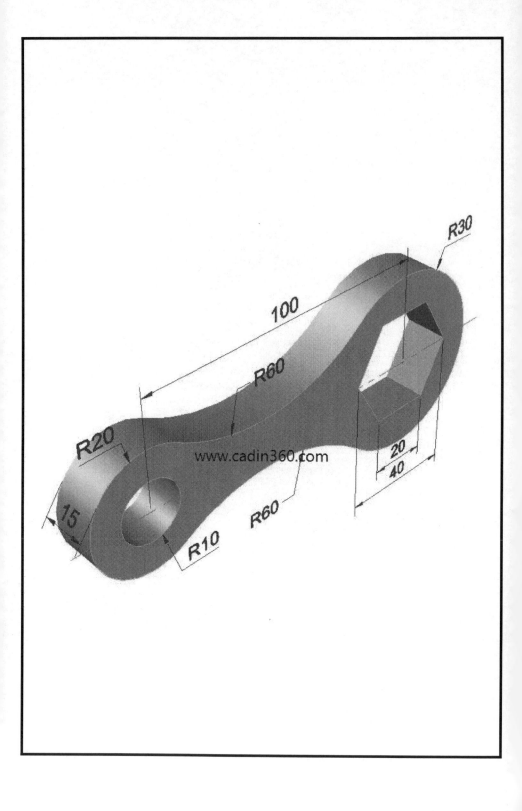

R30

100

R60

R20

15

www.cadin360.com

R60

R10

20

40

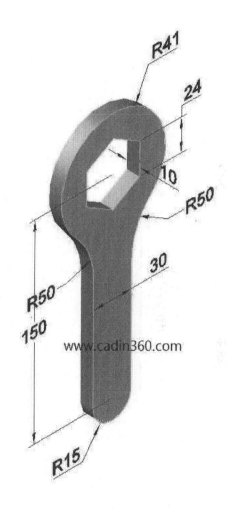

R41

24

10

R50

R50

30

150

www.cadin360.com

R15

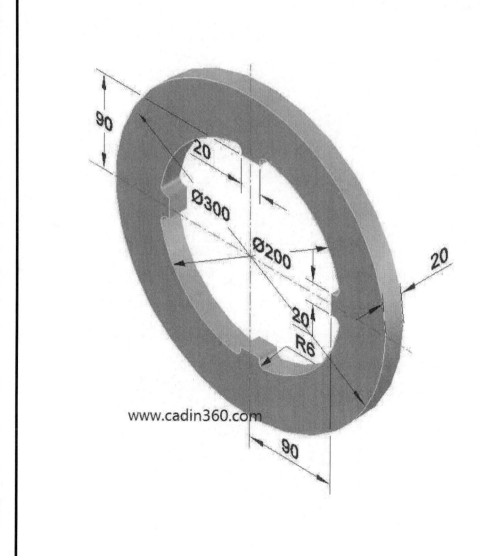

www.cadin360.com

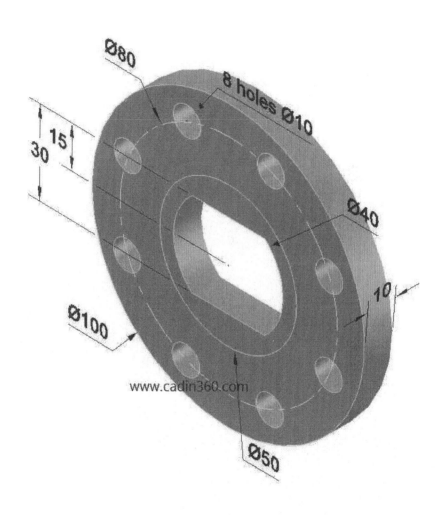

Ø80

8 holes Ø10

15

30

Ø40

Ø100

10

www.cadin360.com

Ø50

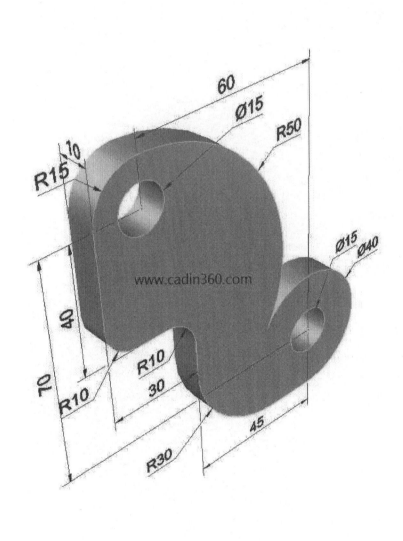

60

Ø15

R50

R15

10

Ø15 Ø40

40

70

R10

R10

30

R30

45

www.cadin360.com

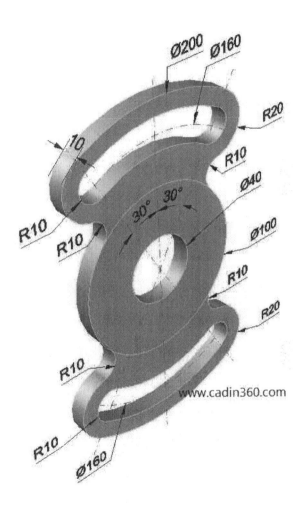

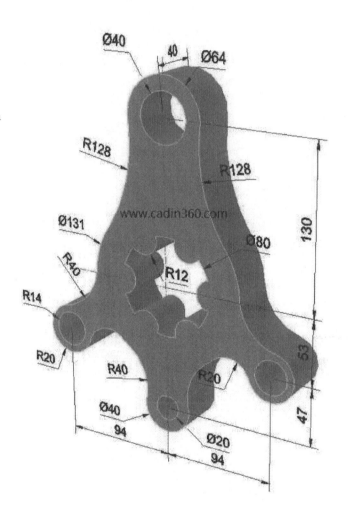

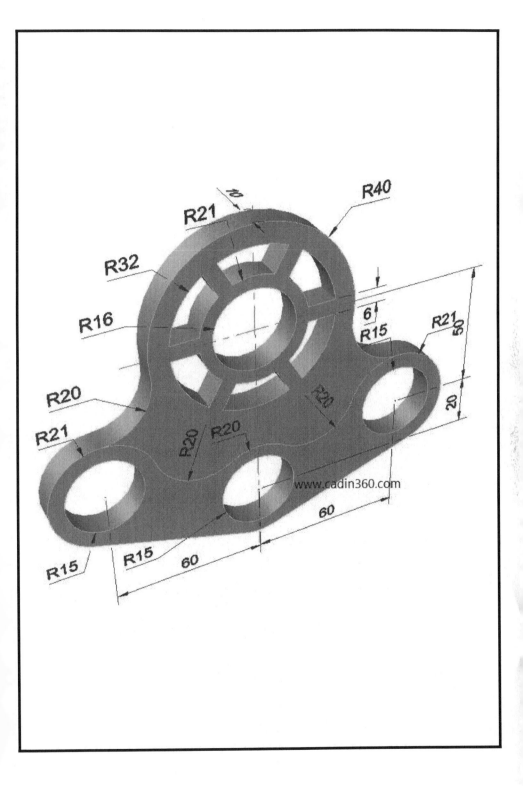

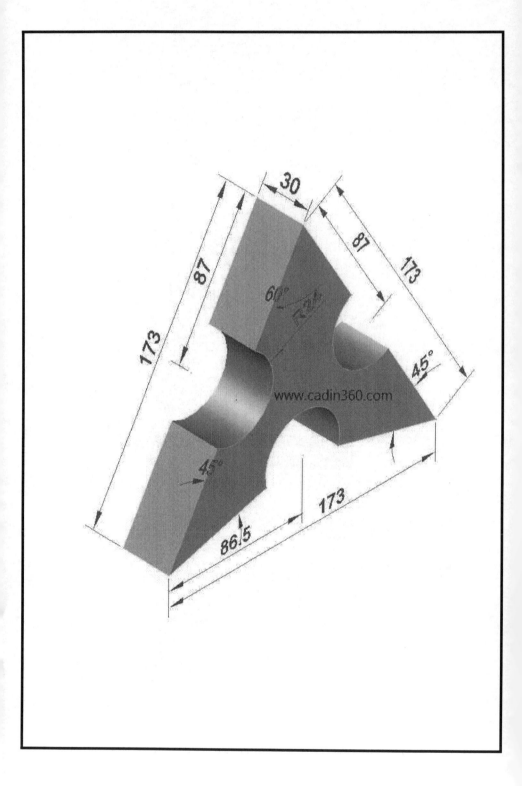

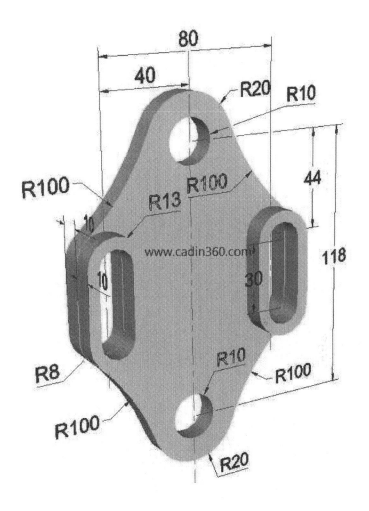

80

40

R20 R10

R100

R13 R100

44

10

www.cadin360.com

118

10

30

R10

R100

R8

R100

R20

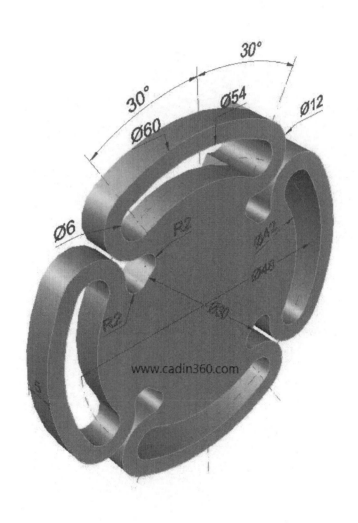

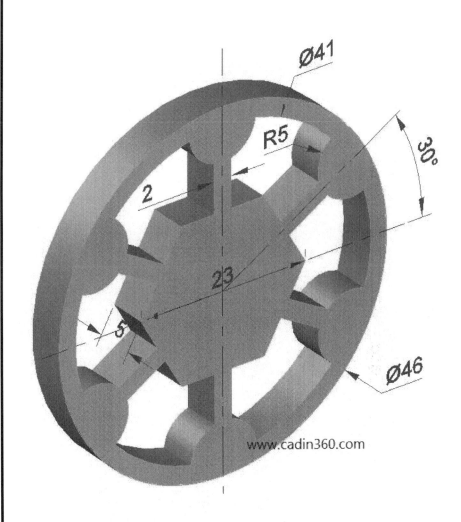

Ø41

R5

2

30°

23

5

Ø46

www.cadin360.com

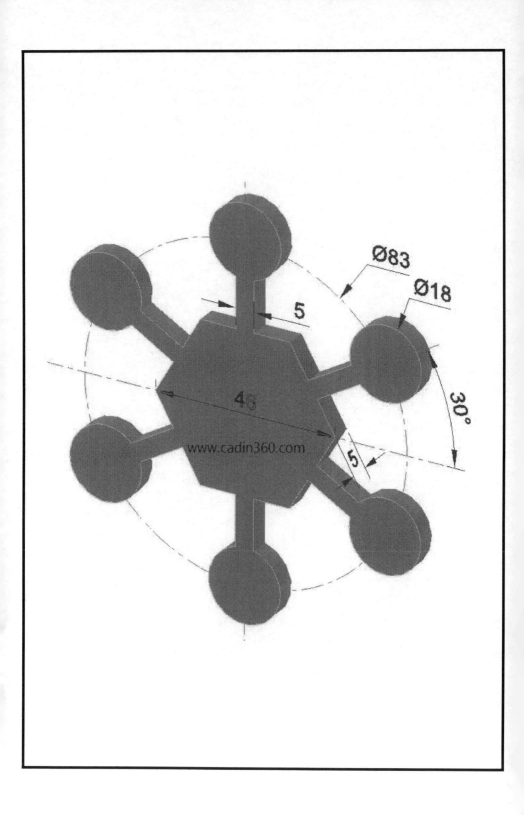

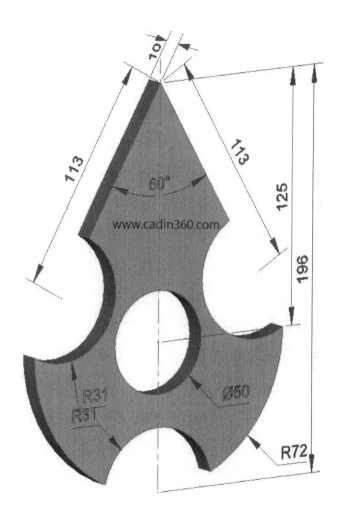

www.cadin360.com

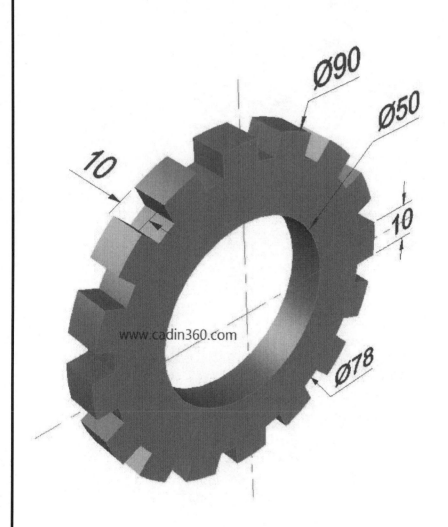

Ø90

Ø50

10

10

www.cadin360.com

Ø78

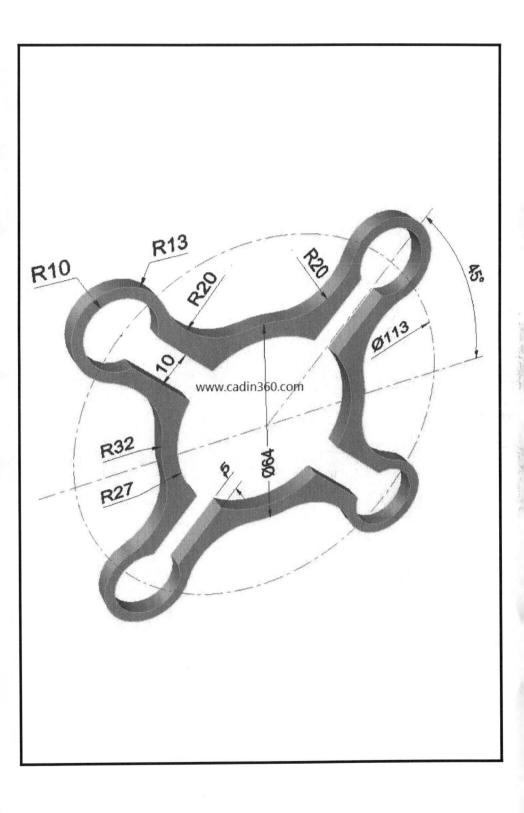

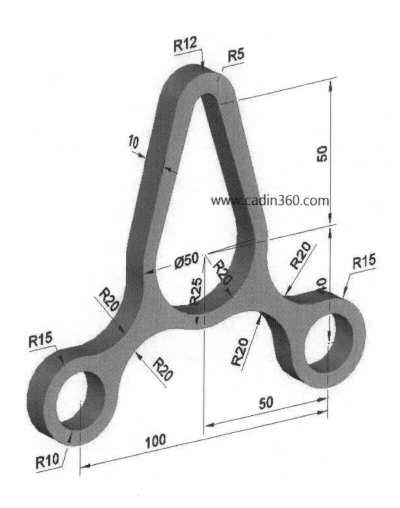

R12 R5

10

www.cadin360.com

Ø50 R20

R25 R20 R15

R20 40

R15 50

R20

R20 50

100

R10

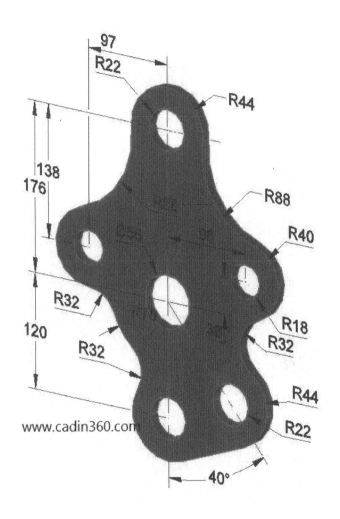

www.cadin360.com

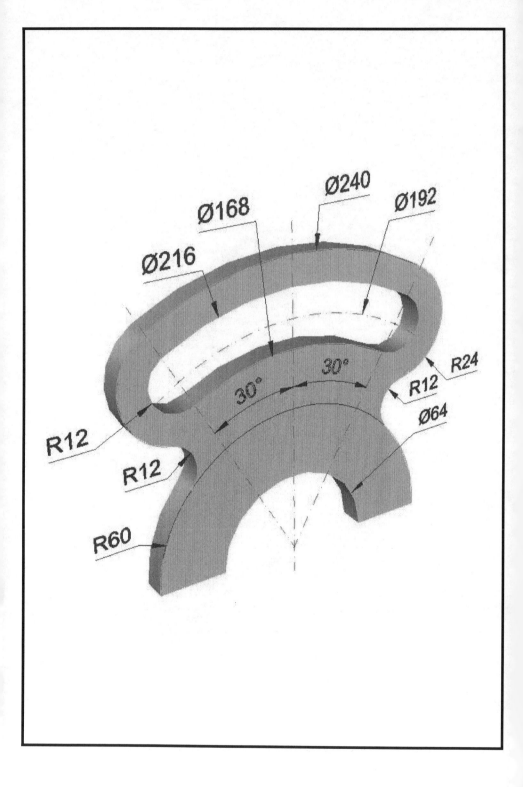

Thank You

Made in the USA
San Bernardino, CA
23 December 2017